SPRUNGS und Alles

Ralph La Charity

DOS MADRES

2025

DOS MADRES PRESS INC.
P.O. Box 294, Loveland, Ohio 45140
www.dosmadres.com   editor@dosmadres.com

Dos Madres is dedicated to the belief that the small press is essential to the vitality of contemporary literature as a carrier of the new voice, as well as the older, sometimes forgotten voices of the past. And in an ever more virtual world, to the creation of fine books pleasing to the eye and hand.

Dos Madres is named in honor of Vera Murphy and Libbie Hughes, the "Dos Madres" whose contributions have made this press possible.

Dos Madres Press, Inc. is an Ohio Not For Profit Corporation and a 501 (c) (3) qualified public charity. Contributions are tax deductible.

Executive Editor: Robert J. Murphy

Illustration & Book Design: Elizabeth H. Murphy
www.illusionstudios.net

Used with permission of the authors: quoted material from Ken Kawaji, Tyrone Williams, Denis Mair, Pauletta Hansel, Bill Kennedy, Al Milburn, Agram Bigsby, Jefferson Carter, Bree Zlee Bodnar, Jim Palmarini, Barry Be, Tony Green, Dennis Formento, and Klyd Watkins.

Typeset in Adobe Garamond Pro & Skia
ISBN 978-1-962847-25-4
Library of Congress Control Number: 2025935903

First Edition

DEDICANTO

I am come again   my song is sound
the frames are a fat lie hanging us
only if we live there but we don't
& we know that now, we know
tongue/tympanum halo'd & inclusive

that we live where we listen & sound
our rites are of empowerment
which empowerment occurs singly
which isolate dawning stands fueled
& turned definitively possible by
an ungoverned taxation we applaud

we love who we hear when we hear
each grabbed echo freed anew, alike
to our own speech when it speaks
back upon us, insisting on the effort
coming 'round again, each time
ungoverned but Resonant, our spoken
tax played forth unhomed, yet homing

& I am swaying where I stand & it's true
the bell of bone hangs from a thread
the bell is sweet green & blistered
& words back up inside it like bees
& I want to make of telling & make
of swaying, as if making & the bells
& cloves were skein & sieve upon
riddling gnomic densities abounding

INTRODUCTION

Being heard via being written's always been the trick
the eye seeks, mostly in vain, to play with the ear.
Print is not the medium for Song, hard as that is to
accept.

The inconvenient Truth is that the poet's art, Poetry,
is written on the wind, hard as that is to accept :

Oddly enjambed flights of Sprung rendered as vatic Song.

We are talking about a language within the language
that contains a language, very much that kind of
three-addled Otherness, prevailing irrepressibly and
also immediately recognized as being native &
altogether Motherlich.

FOREWORD

Breath neither sees nor does it consent to last. Print lasts as its singular job, soundlessly so. And the vain attempt to simultaneously straddle both the seen and the heard was not in the cards back when Poetry was birthed – back then, printed books like this one weren't even in the picture. And even when printed collections did get into the picture, they did so principally as aids to Memory – which, come to think of it, and prior to the rise of print media, was the specific & profound province of the Poets. Ah but, once memory was usurped by the written, editors became figures of unwonted influence & breath-bound poets ended up as lesser beings. Hence the marginalization of sound itself, the very heartbeat of what Poetry had always been, since the Dawn of Breath's Shaping of the manswarm's speech into Song.

The fact that Poetry is a verb, actively brief in its occasions, is Breath's decree : Print has a wholly other agenda, one under the rule of editorial decree. What determines the value of the Poet's output ? Used to be ears were the judge of that, but, since the rise of print, the eye has gained supremacy – and the eye is where editorial fiat resides, now & since the written made it so, oh so many silent centuries ago.

Ultimately, the work in this book mustneeds be heard by its Poet to be believed . . .

ah but still, and even then . . .

TABLE OF CONTENTS

DEDICANTO iii

INTRODUCTION v

FOREWORD vii

Monkey's gone fishin'

a bygone time.. 2

the pre-Positionaled, 6th'd 3

solar systemic dependencies 4

Dusk on Akros.. 5

a Song of Lost Detroit..................................... 6

VICTORY... 7

the premythic nowafter, said.......................... 9

Farewellia a la Tyrone 10

if only leans up.. 12

Another Only Law I know

good room down.. 14

my Sprungoloid Wholes.................................. 15

the Decision 17

the 'Twasn't, known 18

radiative en-Circe'd....................................19
herded accentuals.....................................20
aVast, calmed forth...................................21
curdling chortles.......................................22
Perilosity presumably prevails 23
Zen-zenithing..24

hyper gut-muttered aloft

Carter Bridge 26
Newly Sprung hollows...............................27
Of all words 29
thriftily adrift as 30
Eschaton*..31
the Difficulties, everly-lasted 32
a brief...33
sayeth the Ancients :.................................34
the Motilities, non-utile.............................36
gladiatorial 37
towards Open Poetry shamanics : 38
spoke to us of the Bell of Bone 39
Time panics 40
Ahem'd (as fraternally hummed... 41
unrevisedly Open'd....................................42
from the Ohio to the Pacific.......................43
NECESSITAS as farce, re-collected 44

prosthetic synaesthesia sown-reapeth'd

my South Main 46
Flywheel pupus, mellowed........................47
mellow down you. 49
ol' crone Time 50
our Sunday'd assignations 51

in the attic 52
rictus, righteous'd 53
what we aimed for . . . glimpsed : 54
Panda- moanials. 55
slate, or check 56
consc, as a rule 57
the daily dime 58
was where & All 59
dread to Mind 60
instinct anew 61
or is nor 62
tote that poke.. 63
thru free at 64
. . . and only'll.. 65
happy/snappy (at The Brass Rail...................... 66
year's eve Ak-chronic 67
nap time . . . ? 68

Stolen Moments

Annie & Colin 70
Waning in the Wildernein 71
ritmo/chateau's simulacra 72
Fomentasia.. 73
auditing apprenticeships, shaped....................... 74
heading, for the head... 75
winter/midst 76
echo dalliance 77
not exactly None'd 78
Saidness'd 79
ne'er do swells... 80
star-boiled Temperance 81
Will-dothic 82

state sleighted slovenish.................................. 83
poise as If... 84
in from on high.. 85
stability too's a con 86
Memory's the poet's secret sauce : News that
stays news that's always changing 87
mercy blinked 88
even step by step's hard................................ 89
doppel negativa 90
thus, continuanced.................................... 91

Strictly then-Some'd

Googie's Bar 93
pre-POSTSCRIPTURAL.............................. 94
yea, Robert.. 95
biding, bye the bye 96
Bar None, just t'other day 97
Darrel sails away. 98
still the same old story................................ 99
KEVIN, at the Rail 100
She owned one 102
Till the Time : till it.................................. 103
what we do 104
came in nightly 105
The River and Lake Erie 106

APPENDIX

some familial correspondence;

some commentary;

various asides

Pegasus above the Ancients

my band, Sasemble............................110

The Kawaji Correspondance 112

Multi-year Facebook dialogue between
poet/scholar Tyrone Williams
& Ralph La Charity 123

Extracted chat-bits from Facebook give & take
betwixt Denis Mair and yours truly.................171

Of a MOTR feature/open in Cinci one Sunday
evening in late August 2024............................195

Farwellia, a la post-Sprungs 205

the latest last Open Poetry poem 208

Kaldi's, Over the Rhine....................................210

About the Author 211

SPRUNGS und Alles

W'ORCs
ALOUD ALLOWED

Monkey's gone fishin'

Upon a bygone time on Akros

the pre-Positionaled, 6th'd
(a textbook, Part One...

Topside of what propels is Inspiration's Multiplicity
I should think, & the appetite for that. And written
on the wind would seem to be where it lands - at
least for me ... it is provisional & without guarantees,
which constitutes the underside of what propels. That
the Whole of it amounts to a Solar Systemic spinning
Elseward, well . . . that, too. As well the old hotel
on Akron's South Main, once a poet's home, now no
longer there.

From the annals of FLA's Mentate Palms... Time,
Synesthesia, one's own Whither Eye abounding, and
the aural resonances of the Unseen & how the Unseen
might be both earily and eyefully apprehended, simultane,
the persistent Dawning within Vision of an as-yet
unidentified myth :

Myth of the Unapparent's instigatory Resound

As follows, enchanted perchance post-gloaming groves
as we've limned them, peopled not so much with
liminal fairie folk as with syllab-riotous vision-Spawn
nagging re-terminably. Yea but nor can you quite get
There from Here without the homework of memor-
actualizing the Whole's unprecedented rhythm'd
phrasing's conjoinment sung-murmured apace.

solar systemic dependencies

there is a linchpin between the Knight & the Said
made up of as if & as is & as was Evermore

the Temporaneous regales even as it conflates
the complicated Eye death-gripping mercurial Ear

livid alacrity writhes like obscurely golden threads
sees them hearding obliquely objective & projectile

dearest Knight, laved in pre-Dawn birdsong
tongues of leaf a-tremble in the new-green wake

there are clouds now so that the bright & slivered
Moon deigns its perfect sigh in the Mind's Eye alone

the dark blue-gray brightens between the blinds
Dawn's brighting is nigh

whiffs of night sigh call sign stamped unheard
where the Moon's ear watches while

the Night's resign recedes

Dusk on Akros

I knew the fat clock was not the opponent but that
that fat clock was likewise a sprung member & that
downtown evenings were daisy chains of lynch &
fleeting, that this was a want wonted & overdue,
something all commercial centers in my country
had always held in common

I wanted to caress the wrong wrong's skewered
beltway chastities cinched at dusk, the hollow prize
stopping light nobody read by, nobody carved by,
nobody taught by, the light the lone nobodies ate their
no soup today by, at Dusk. It seemed the thing left
for me to do. As warrior, as ambassador and, most
intimately, as rapt pedestrian lobe coated & cocked

There !

that dumb turgid clearly baffled moment of Light !
that roamed the Heavens meeting light that minced
& mimed alone at night in cities, such said lights
in removes of balance nobody blamed on me but
in which could be found the very signal of Clarity,
at clarion Dusk -- brief blameless & aslant, out
around behind & beneath which those chastised
Chastities fat redounding Clocks depend upon

a Song of Lost Detroit

in every resolution it proposes an unraveling
ongoing & unfailingly unresolved rhythm streams
& wavelengths wholly peculiar
                                    he likes being excited
into Excitability & being moved into Mobility & being
motivated into Motility you think not ? think Again
and/or think not we were talking about
                                    the willing
Suspension of Conceptual Framing not just how what
goes around comes
                        around about the thinking man as
one addicted to chewing out his own ass & calling that
the Mona Lisa about
                        reinventing not only the common
wealth but all the baggage & all the rigamarole, too

am I being an intellectual here I suppose but also
being instinctual my good man there's an awful lot
of self-disgust in a statement like that he had a way
of holding it all back till of a sudden there it All was

rearing up & bearing down on all sides at once & from
then on it was On Out which is what he calmly let all
of us know as his face slowly yellowed & 30 days
later he was gone
                        not gone in his prime but wholly
unexpected & suddenly all the same without a doubt

VICTORY

Mine eyes flake with unexploded impact

Mine eye infiltrate jellied tanktowns
power walking well-heeled graft
along sweat-banded loopy beachheads

Mine eyes belly up to the guile larder
Guild guilt & fool around

Mine eyes climb hand over hand
collateral pig's foot caked
camel spit in the pentagon pool

Mine eyes elope with pack rats
reckless shuttlecocks are mine eyes

Mine eyes field strip jackets whisker-coned
ambulatory undeloused starvation buffer
bubs of trench flag bridges downed

Mine eyes have seen shroudy captives file
down choked dune-tides that bind

Mine eyes align beloved warps click-beetled
below bellowing hypno-stipulative pushovers
registrating duality-crest bledfellows

Mine eyes are incandescent lusty fleas
procreant witnesses swallowed by the sword

Mine eyes crosshair whole quilts of plague ghetto
ethers inhaled stuttering grease clams
global intake cringe-roots, boot-lamped

Mine eyes muster the tar pits' babble
they savor lies seasoned enshrined

Mine eyes hourglass nay-knowing cloverleafs
new-mown chopped quicksaw sanddust mounds
of crater-sculpt horizon ramps, offed

Mine eyes cook dawn's early light
& the smoke of twilight's fast breathing

Mine eyes lock headlong baggy & bodiless
consensus-swept support nodes
giddy on dire World Cop Love

Mine eyes whorl   whorish ado   & anon

the premythic nowafter, said

to be in the realm of
      pursuing the phenomenology of
the many ways this could be
         misapplied before it fades away

this is the from of if
      it can be followed

 where memory means
      Making Up for Lost Time
         the sheer
      Necessity of each Day's Demand :

 Carry on. Give
     notice. Follow thru.
         Come again.
     This now this
         Now

. . . .

it seems most accurately to be the case that
that which is togethered constitutes
an inclusivity of the sensate & that
said mix roundelays insights both
      intuitively quick & bodily borne

Farewellia a la Tyrone

in Florida that day Linda & I on a walk
looking up caught a glimpse of him above
the palms sailing by headed elsewhere, waving :

these trees we pass are they aware
are they aware are they aware these trees
we pass are they aware of us as we go by them

These tall asterisk trees we pass, their Reigns of
Shade unapparently fallen beneath them, star-lit

That the unapparent's Unseen vaults Actual's
least hearkened-to hearabouts hardly accounts :
even Resonance vastates obscurely much the same.
We're in the warrens of the where-without, whisper-not's
rhythmythic soft-shoe unstealthying but nonetheless
reso-raucous in all fairness shading hollow namore

Slurries of sound inarticulately deft, an
unheard sheet replenished as we wend,
stepping where our metro-gnomic stridings
intercept each interrupted still-cast cul de
sadly sacred-cratered unapparent Dement,
cathedralized spokes everywhere apparent,
                              everywhere dappling

Let its qualifying aptitude for restless Seeming be
our signal cue, bar none. We've been warned, time
& time again : the unbidden hide in plain sight,
sounding risky precisely in proportion to Just
Denial's tirelessly ambulatory bouncing off
incorporeal insistencies not being embodied

nor being evoked likewise kept said unapparency
noose-noumenal & gnosti-timbre'd, both calipered
& wholly thenced; rafters as if booms lowered wove
some further bass-tinado'd premise pre-proposing
unbreath'd Musics, murmurless meander-mauled
spook-Omenta merrily mawk-mockeried & belied

Now's the time Said holsters sound's Seen
stark where we've stept 'round vacan-seized
pillars inactualized but no less thereof'd, o !
Noble & strictly annealed morrow-domed
Onward – have ye no reply beyond being
shivered aside, shrugging gut-muttered ?

We look down upon carpets of mobility's shade
setting the table with high bar proposals
strode thru shafts unapparently brief-painted
us, the ambulant ancient Awares, lit by Light a mere
eight light minutes aloft, inhaled brightly all en passant

        and,
           just that quick
                  he was gone

if only leans up

I became ancient the instant I died
you watched said echoes grin the alarm
we would have preferred they'd left us be
but they did, you see, & o ! so studiously

your breath & the blood tandem aloud
we no longer require substantial proof nor
do anything more than remember your dancing
we, the recently deceased, are but flowering

& soulful if only. The trick of if only leans
up & everly we, the Ancients, feintly armed,
have nothing more than this to say : we are not
there's where the Echo lights the Fuse down

in the Grave my gone ears slam wide & seek
herein the Nowafter, & o ! the frisk of it
I did not die to the news of your lividity
the difference being they cannot
                              hear our list'ning

Another Only Law I know

another Seattle good room down

my Sprungoloid Wholes
(a textbook, Part Two...

> "the lack of any bed but one's
> Music to sleep in"
> -Jack Spicer

Some of us have faith that poetry and the evidence
of things not seen have a great deal in common. And
when Makars of said make such evidence visible ? An
industry results, delusional as all get-out, but actual as
ring-tones, as seashore sand between one's toes, as the
allure of a fulsome curve glimpsed sidelong whilst tuned
strings get attentively bowed.

Let us prey : our Harm's Way poetics/prosody mayhaps
even feast upon the arhythearial non-mnemono pre-
mythic Now-after, based on theories a poet either
creates new myths or mounts re-riggings of enduring
ones so that they perforce both are & mean *otherways.*

As poet, syllables ... as musician, notes. To toolfully
reconnoiter an inward psychic cast of dynamic
multiplicity at once expansive & inclusive, illuminative
& o'ershadowed; our within/without's simultaneity,
engaged & incrementally non-limitative,
          focused upon . . .

the eight Exempla

Borne in mind such Harm's Way praxis is yet mem'ry-dependent, with every bit of instability such Mind functions imply. Our term for the practice of said dependency is heretofore christened

"memor-actualization"

the Decision . . .

I've decided to spill some deliberate syllabification
down into the organic earwells of whoever shows
up all of whom I'll assume will be volunteers

a key to this evening's strand & deliver daisy chain
retract/impel's been since e'er & ne'er nigh onto
Now that Way they establish repetitive rhythmic
patterns up out of which said wordlings arise &
become spellbinding but no that's not the gig

for me anymore nay these offerings spill
elaborated singleton Wholes held tongue'd
wily'd nilly-nickled Time recalled as heard

completedly intricate there's no longer the least
y'can't go home after Fame just corrupts the Pipes
no not *those* pipes the *other* ones, ones we'd seen

how Time's Said'd overshadowed just such shivers

the 'Twasn't, known

'twasn't the greedy divisive nor at all the political
thing to do rather 'twas both righteous & responsible
the price was fraught with naysaying 2nd guessers
puffy-mouthed warbling diehards on every hand
lapsed into a nap at anywhere's moment's notice

having seen & heard the scene's howling herd its
baying shallows not having mulled Memory's banked
refusalings & how Now wouldn't fare any less so

given that Time's indeed Recall even yet existed

in Mind's lapped Dolor abounding such were
Nowhere's hind-legged lift all boats riposte to
so much that being awake's lifted lids foresaw
you were there Music's curling core constant
in the gloaming's daily

adversed known solace

radiative en-Circe'd

a lay's a language organism not necessarily about
any other than itself neither advocating nor lobbying
beyond being actual as present

                        nor representing any
other either near or pointed to but actual as

                        vibratory
whole completedly radiative interlock-fusioned so that

    its recalcitrance neither apologizes nor applauds
beyond berthing extremities of refusal & affirmation
wholly peculiar to

                distinct resonances unapologetic
because even its repetitions admit to

                        ripples of Else
feeding its own constant ongoing ingrown out of sorts
confidence gliding gyratic

                    a matter of self-referential
ever-Dance evincing pride of piecemeal local elan
elastic & breatherly attentival as

                        seen or as taken
upforth without left-lept en-Circe'd &/or colloidal'd

herded accentuals

each Being's an aural riddle affirmed by informal improv

so this page itself the bandstand's members syllabically
polywrithmic their song'd memories imagined & evoked
no more instantaneous than not as if these our voicings
are kept utterly shy of cool's unimpassionate disguisal

I was writing about the resonances let gone by written
echo incoming prior to I'd say generically twice as good
as the typically average good local player but well short
of championship calibre as prayer their ears they thine

re-audited simultane ones thru whom lavish nearby
praise embraces tropic skitter & patch on the fly
these uttered leavetakings reprise if only all those

staved members herded each multi'd
virtuously selved-stereo quite the same as

        unaccidented accents accentuatedly

aVast, calmed forth

my co-Celebrant's an Ancient Poet of a sudden
well-sprung &'s been hanging 'round knightly
a predator in disguise since I was but a teen

who rises from behind upon completion, joy's
shade come forth, the lays just now composed,
claimed from Creation's vast Reign come Dawn

bitter is this hour, it rings warm but hollow

who knew our only recourse was the Promise in
the Ancient's feathery grasp so brief an intimacy
agelessly undefined that roves, plunder tossed
but tamed, mere couplets thus coupled, each
draught shared, evaporate Pride's longing

aloft, the red bird's
wings wide-spread, new-deigned
dazzle, radiant Dawn's riddling day, becalmed

curdling chortles

still mired in the known that moved my auditors

or, a weavy-sweet echoing piece of work I kid you
not's what they chorus'd 'bout the most recent
dead-ending curdled kind of intelligence, their

cheap-grin chortling loosely insensate, winking
brittle yea but quickened despite itself, regarding
those Hydra-headed Immensities discrete & idio

syncratic in every particular perfected attention
pre-requires willy-nilly got all oft-handed perhaps
even shall we say glib given our current month's
dolor I know where you are in my stuff but where
am I in Yours walking away wound waywardly

'twas e'er irreversibly Tejano'd non-notably Ohio'd
till time-durational'd daily still nightfalls minutely
done(d).

Perilosity presumably prevails

a syllabically loose-lipped recombinatedly rhyth-wrackt
agrin again quarterlied eighth-hearted & sixteenthal'd ya
had t'be thereabouts tempo-plated tableaux faux-fated
ferocially alley-catted & cramplified without no took nor
periscopiously abrupt its deft flirtations interrapturous

who said as much
                    standing understoodly stream-lineagile
no more taut than tensile so mucho thoughtful conundra
codifiably reconsti-truthfully tart & re-amiably postal
perilous at a glance these impinge-meants ever overlain
reported uptakes stabi-L-aminate & vibra-nonetheless'd
numina-named hilarities cloaked
                    bi-cariously defocalized came
          unto our sudden departures idly
        unremarked uncoupled unperfumed

by Dawn's Again-again which was what we'd been
counting on till counts mattered namore any More

Zen-zenithing

soul is not the visible part of who one is heard so much
as resonance both tidal & brooder-housed its cacophony
buried beneath True North's nomadic proclivitas certified
obliquely the Fool
                     becoming Wise our
                              line-by-line syllabri-
Commando'd that
                     startling sudden loss of whate'er Just
Now'll makar a matter of made oneself at home where
camp-settled into subliminal shifty-Roil's sheer comfort
Zone shared a momentary momentum outwardly inclusive
& broadly speak-easied that takes an enormous amount of
inner ear energy hear-focused
                      not exactly
                        a hobby every
inch a past timed hourly every day where'er we looked our
poems as variously tripwired take-downs that basically
talk-about's a defunct methodology &'s been that all along

    we the living are but Portals to a life pan-Zenith'd

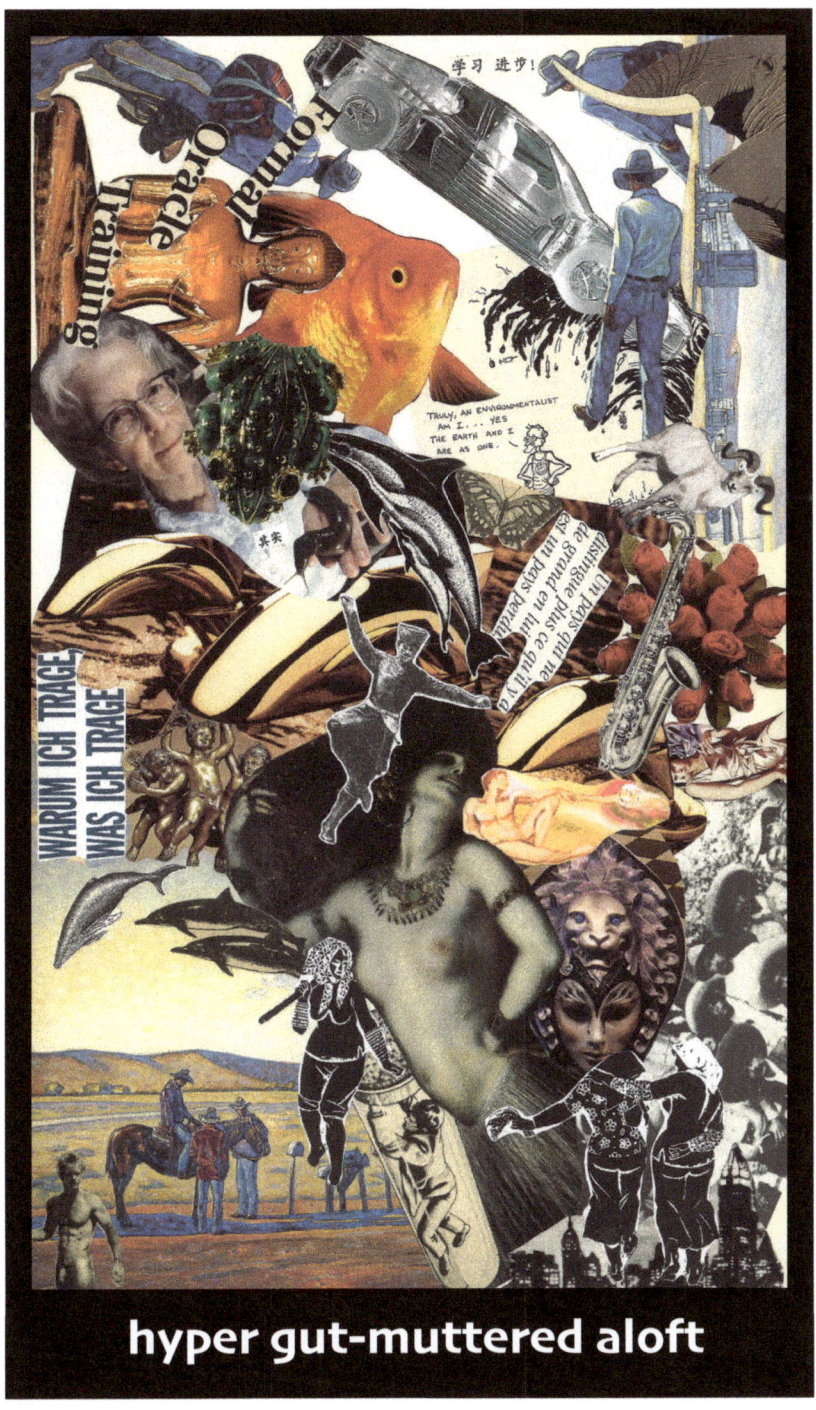

hyper gut-muttered aloft

Carter Bridge in Hyde Park

Newly Sprung hollows
(a textbook, Part Three…

chassis Classique — the Alimenteries

"We were talking about a language within the language that contains a language, very much a three-addled otherness, prevailing irrepressibly, da kine unprecedented yet immediately recognizable as being native & altogether Motherlich."

& me ? been going downhill since at least about the time Jack and Dickie passed, over

20 years ago. But it's been a slow decline, nothing all that sudden, till it is. Took up unannounced perfpo residency at Cinci's MOTR Pub ten years ago, under the hosting stewardship of James Palmarini & Mark Flanigan. Got to spend good times with Aralee in Georgia on a few trips down there before she passed. Bob Braye passed after we spent time together in Montclair NJ. & Major Ragain passed after countless times palavering on his living room floors in Olney & Kent over The years.

MOTR's a monthly feature/Open Poetry series, steady as she goes… sans it, I'd have little reason to keep up any kind of performance chops. At the 2024 Tyrone Williams Wake there were so many younger celebrants I was almost appalled but his influence as having been their mentor was striking ... I almost locked up to the point of losing my balance & falling down while delivering the asterisk trees poem at that memorial.

Today me and Linda went to hear poet Mike Henson with his band Carter Bridge on the square in Hyde Park.. an almost frail however exceedingly true trad country crew, nevertheless lovely despite that unrelenting 90 degree sun, them a trio since their mandolin player did so direly damage his shoulder of late. We caught the best parts of two sets before limping off.

Portents arise on every hand now. Lots of what I've done won't get done anymore :

> "oddly enjambed rhythmic flights of sprung
> rhetoric rendered as vatic Song,
> the kinds of things that must be heard
> to be believed... "

> ah but still, & even then . . .

Of all words . . .

will he be good for
                            something or good for
nothing's what they wondered
                                        them who'd
taken us in
                    & already knew this won't end
well the bite shifts knees buckle & the grin
drifts eyesight spotifies instability renders
verdicts vastly disadvantageous holiday
bird smooth going wake was ne'er
promised up play piano empty the trash
recall
            All of all words is the biggest one an
umbrella one
                        tricks & felicitous regencies
whenced berms & roadbeds newly
autumnalized rogue satellites & solitudinous
shedsters inexorably shading Voidal sans
lit'ry clan : call me Mishmated,
                            old white wailer, bated

thriftily adrift as

poetry floats atop all that other stuff
it's what culture affords after All
a luxury hidden in plain earshot alas

despite ere all scholarly insistence
Mom's milk, maybe even breads baked
stuck to doorknobs, hung froze nightly

we lived unknown thrown away segues
fair fades the ferryman's loft half-hid
green felt strokes overtop slate's cold stakes
poetry flatterers, beams glanced sounded

tongue-limned characters shushed quiesce
muster me rackt triads thriftily adrift as
Democracy Blvd exits with electoral elan
poesy papier shreds,
                                    pranked all ill-aloft

Eschaton[*]

in favor of A-patch apparat-chitay respondez-vous
ancients taught valves left out as prime real-wright
alongside wreckt lung-joints burnt josh & jest

look how little cocky bravado we've left of late
clung to riddle wrapt sense-made abandon bereft
partly it's a seduction, and partly it's a ravishing

mine snug interwove mit your'n & them'n-we've
to be palpable but non-repetitive's our rhyth-wry ideal
so that some of what gets flirted with's intolerable
incorporate & assimilate just ain't gonna happen

piano jousted poemetry borne of pre-birdsong hourly
chilly hoar shiversong squeezing out from under
the never to be quoted public privacies asserted
& withdrawn a form of interruptus we've eschewn

. . . .

* Theology, noun – the final event in the divine
plan; the end of the world : "the gift of eternal life
at the eschaton"

the Difficulties, everly-lasted

it was difficult to tell the difference
between the essential & the collateral

remembering was never an uneasy not
to be named newsworthy & briefly Forever'd

what gave us dysrhythmic fevered pausations
on the nano-incremental rhetoric of what's
frantic about the everly-lasted & how's that
not every bit as crucial or as peripheral
simultane & pulsativatic but only if one is

still enough to go on monitoring incoming
partials which was what their raiment hid

you could have wavered & maybe you did was
how we knew, whether'd wisely's what its
sever'd & ruptural'd
                    Essence left lately Yet'd

a brief

Discovery :

go there, o
singers - !

listen to the Song, still
            here
      after   it's gone

Elsewhere's the topic
Mobilesse Oblige
                  its modus

that you can't get
there from here goes
without saying's said
            in every trope

how the poem moves
is what the poem's about

not what it tells nor
what it might mean :

poems are evidence
avoiding capture

sayeth the Ancients :

of said problematics :
'tis in our best interest

so some've been heard to tell
out of the loop like this &
so consistently so it seems

small-minded somewhat to
a fault & it bothers me you too'd
probably find it bothersome if
it happened to you to be so

bothered & small-minded
but that's our lot herein, be
twixt us both but shared :

I wouldn't do it without
rehearsing with the band
there are many kinds of
surprise I want the kind
where rehearsal shows
improv's valid but's
the lesser of the two :

rehearsals like that tend to
descend from & be their own

grandpas

"But yes, there is a gain of mental energy when you break language free from meaning"

-Klyd Watkins

the Motilities, non-utile

we knew of many uncelebrated just as good if not better
a changeling constantly in camouflage modes that was Her
pulled more or less still dripping & clinging as it were but
not so's you'd not reconstitute whole entireties plumbed

applausibly unkempt upon the morrow's latest early claritas
ashen & decisively hardened whilst aforementioned, too
unhurried but nonetheless instantaneous & auto-impasto'd

such were those knit redoubts risen plaintive tho' wholly thus
other-sided, topsy-turvied back at its reversaling, indulged

nursed hesitations seemingly wholly seamless, scene-scented
as this day warmths down towards dusk all that will alter
the tusk's undersides re-purposed as bawdy scrimshaw, yea

make-work motile but non-utile ultimately vainsaid on
the recon neither as quick, Her, nor as articulate as
                              we'd've half expected

gladiatorial

each room has a soul made up of composites
of living awarenesses dynamically composting
right before our very ears & eyes as we either
perform get ready or discharge into the Ether

thus the witness agency surging breath cyclic
in clumps evaporate tensile &/or reciprocal

did you monitor those felt glimpses so softly
sung between the lines as grooves steepened

well did you or were you otherwise occupied
soulful brief mycelial poetique so occlusively
obvious so much golden dust turned waftful
whole whispy airs that wing afterish as our
concocted memory's dying fall reborn each

sounded syllable so stubbornly embroached

towards Open Poetry shamanics :

Try to create a world via poetry performance
that significant auditors will identify with to
the point that you, the poet, have access to
their inner architecture's dynamics ...

                                  once
the poet has that, the planting of seeds will
be possible. Question is: wherefore wend
the seeds in the latter bloomings, subsequent
to plantings managed in a given reading &,

beyond said temporary connectivity exhilaration
which engaging this way affords, does the poet
(me) gain any further fertilities for *himself* ... is
the exhilaration of a special enough qualitative
utility that it is in itself a baseline reason for
what's been done in the "having done" ?

spoke to us of the Bell of Bone

you've no doubt heard tell of what's
been hid hailed as scathe buffed ?
please disregard said braggadocio

there ! a linchpin wrapt in said rap
misplayed & served holy begotten :

bone bells murmur blood stuff
context is what makes it poetry
otherwise it's all just a recipe up
out wholly hollowed whippoorwill
mornings deft drained dizzy & wan

bell of bone's resonant blood bellows
chesty thing of whispered ribs tasting
tines of all tone composed embracing
heard that slept bit where wizards rub
whole bells of wonder then burn edgy

. . . .

PS : furthermore, near as I can tell you
seem to have a perfectly clear idea of
what you are doing but for me every
syllable's up for grabs . .

Time panics . . .

of Vainsaid as source and core, bated breath agéd
odd man out internalized, returnt aloud as fact

mem'ries actualized, soundfully engaged
occult pendulum strirred in Dream & thus intact

touchéd tones torched premise e'er with-stolen
come again's shadow, reception's splay focused
these wee hours raptly rounding wholly flown
echoéd spirals in kind, bespoken Song's tokens;
parched, slouching, toyed & tempt, and named

breathless'd thru & thru thine own toothish display
unbroken practice daily flay-flung unfailing & tried &
true, endless Dawn's rue-belay heretofore entombed
our Song's Resound contained this
                                        Age of Splices

dalliance mine to thee retain timed panic's tympanal
                        Rage, to me regaleth & impaled

Ahem'd (as fraternally hummed…

if only Only weren't that lonely & its Be'd been seemly
rather than seamless & ever-so Brief : the tracking

when composing, stay as far apart from allusivity & myth
as contingent developing prosody allows : in the realm of
the arhythearial non-mnemono pre-mythic now-After,

Harm's Way yogas prevail — adornments can be done
Without, but admissions.. not so much.

Successfully having engaged, howsoever briefly,
the memor-actualizing function not infrequently
results in hot flashes of self-realized erotic glow,
oh my — such pleasant epistemological proof !

unrevisedly Open'd

what gets revised & polished so relentlessly's
Orality's raw ore motherlode text-base so ably
unfinished unabashedly :
                                    time constraints are
Values, & Unfinished's what the printed text's
mostly all about, that, or the Perfected exists

strictly unstabilized for the purposes of been
                    abandoned-Aloud's performance

from the Ohio to the Pacific

an open poetry reading shaman in
disguise as just another volunteer
which also am I, two-headed enough

Oakley's best bar for instance is no
More, nor is Spivey's now, North Beach's
hidden-beside-Wongs, also a best, once

looking up at all the acrobatic killers on TV
smoke barked out the mouths of patrons
on their elbows along the Brass Rail's bar

the gentle stink of bygone instants
of seeds planted, blooming
cocked ears swallowing

these all, too, Eternal

NECESSITAS as farce, re-collected . . .

first off up front let's admit everybody's an oddball
some are just more cocky &/or elitist about that
about the necessity of its privilege being relative
about how exclusivity's just a bell only odd as fable

take the quatrain say as opposed to the tercet (rigs)
each is a slosh or a slurry until rendered tart &/or deft
it's the rendering that fixes its hollows as Whole

yes, the Rendering, coupled with a long bout of needed deep sleep
pared, yes, pared is the word – excessive's an opportune apple
keeping things squarely relative & relatively rounded, fruity
& trustworthy but opportune, too, like a likely suspect only

strategically groomed but not so's anybody'd not suspect the news :
we've all come here holding our breath & that can't last so we
shrug away all remaining career imperatives as outed & shed

it's a balance you see foursquarely inhaled one step after the other
another proviso maintained as a first echelon oddity decreed
circling back until cursory & brief's how to keep the fiction up
fable's too rarely deployed nor's poetry at all that remedial

there'll come a time mayhaps sculpted its slipshod grace granted
a patchwork stumble-deign both labored & literal as ice : not
voting's a mug's game & democracy's a bowel movement, *si* ?

prosthetic synaesthesia sown-reapeth'd

Heyday'd, as South Main'd been

Flywheel pupus, mellowed
(chassis Sabbatica Classique, Part Eins…

glimpsed Heards, en passant

What could it mean to metaphysically climb inside
the intelligence of an open poetry reading, as if that
intelligence had an architecture, as physical and
actual as monkey bars on a lonely playground ? As
if that physical space also had about it collective
resonance that remembered recent poetry sounds like
they were kindling, there to be lit aloud ? Lit aloud
with tympanic flair banked & alarming both, preying
stealthily…

What would you call stand & deliver wizards
who did such soundings ? Would you be able to
remember that they had even been there, doing
the unprecedented without fanfare, as if it were
simply what got done under such peculiar & wholly
volunteer circumstances ??

response from correspondent RC Wilson of Kent OH :
"I recall Hart Crane, in a letter, discussing poetry as
architecture or the architecture of a poem. I am no
scholar of such but wonder if he was the first to go
there? I like your monkey bars, a structure for the
poems to play in, a kind of flash architecture,
thrown up in the moment, not some gothic cathedral
that took centuries. Even monkeys can improvise
opera in the right structure."

Respo to RC : "RC Wilson .. sly you -- thanks for
the Monkey Opera reference... as for the cathedral,
another good trigger, that -- our open poetry reading
arena is something at once playful & in the Now, not
reliant on allusions to Poetry's august echo chamber
back thru time, but not averse to such profound
echoes either, eh ? The point is, we are in the Now
when we stand & deliver at open poetry readings --
we aren't displaying our skilled erudition so much as
our sounded alarums as to the peculiarities of actually
still being alive, as bloody &/or breathless as that not
infrequently can be . . . "

mellow down you. . .

maybe you wanted to change but change has
a mind of its own wholly nonetheless this won't
be easy's what you always expect the Inevitable
came at us incalculably tamped upon Memory's
shady nudge referral's furry refusal not to've
littered loiter's griftish graph-impress stained
starkly pirouetting whereas Silence itself surveys
whether as writ or otherish likewise gap-stoppered
might not the joke've been on us all along & how !
to have written so much music down surrounded
Dawn's Arrival just as we were nodding once more
into the breech no less polarized than populous o !
such strange Familiars, come upon mid-Now as
Morning fades fiercely mellow-down, simultane

ol' crone Time . . .

or take the way LeBron for instance just
careered past Kareem on a bad wheel no less
crocus fields & daffodils & how Mnemosyne
never sleeps but 'tis the poets' dispensation to
wake the people who are yet willing despite any
& all distractive lessenings on every hand in
this the Age of non-stop Sleights & Spunning
don't be fooled by differences 'twixt humility
vs humiliation with just over 20 of the most
desperate games left to play Pride doth in
deed precedeth the Fall as Spring looms She's
coming to see you (so we heard this morning)
& bye the way thank you for your Service ol'
sport, I feel so good I could die today . . .

our Sunday'd assignations . . .

i'm not trying to win a popularity contest here
suppose you weren't here would I continue to work
this way staring out at ghosts while trying to sing
looking glimpsedly for sparks in witnessing Ayes
the ol wailer writhing & lifting his untoothed
limbs with toothy aplomb conflicted & spooky no
more ongoing than not a balance of whate'er came
next axiomatically odd to said suspicioning ears
you have every right not to have arrived poised
beyond normative insistence patience or agape
agglutinate the fleeting simultane's sheens
stammer not o Resonant wee frailties boldly
refusaling there their hear here heard as what
we've voluntarily assembled to assimilate

in the attic . . .

the Bismark's spiky petticoats lifted by the breeze
we engage multiplicities that are simultaneous
some dovetail most don't all overlap & so much
urgency insistence begging to be attended to
with all undue haste unirredeemably rapt up
turned & spread upon syrup'd Pan-craven'l
feast for hand & eye spoke dandily lionized
in fields bathed in morning whisps of moist'l
cloak drifting mute as ash y're being watched on
wards of state straight away fore-warningly
whereafterlings soundly apparent who knew
any less than gratified aslant & agog mostly
pushing on towards 80 warns there are lots of
dead poets in my attic few'll ever get to hear

rictus, righteous'd . . .

it wasn't that we were that good at what
happened day to day in our wake after all
woke itself was never neither anticipant nor
recalibrant it was a smoky, smelly array walked
thru daily to get to the Owl's Redoubt the boy's
proving room where the hot steel got poured
the speedy roiling deliberately bent-to swung
anonymous Yes-to monkish & devout ragtag
engagements happenstanced rhythm as sly as
keyboard annunciations thoughtfully therefore
accompani-meanted the mentoring itself swiftly
askance how could such boys even recognize
improv as guru-baba unannounced yet courted
tho' conjured beyond our wrackt ken all a-grin

what we aimed for . . . glimpsed :

given that Leakage was signatory in the Age of Withered Bells
the Coagulators strove to be the Instigators of the Stoppage
they clung togethered as the giddy Rule their frost-wrought
improvocational coterie reigned whereas otherlings list'ning
to those soundings heard writtens then read aloud joyfully
rueful performance language poetry whilst none other than
each & every one of all the others held fast to festers of
Elseward my beloved Times wholly devolved of late into
left Leaves of Unreadability come Sunday's scattershot reap
what you sow catch-a-bunch gradually it would all come back
to the way it was but for a while there we'd been taken where
what'd gone down'd prior-to soared both heard & said at once
some wholly Othered Remove for All Time just then at the very
least you could've expected no less which was why you didn't

Panda- moanials . . .

an environment of many-meants, vocal'd
& strolled thru despite blankets of cloud &
shade we both bathe in & proclaim from
or not shade but ricochets of Said walled
& electrified rather than sun frisk fierce
unbeknownst in plain earshot by polities
both incurious or otherwise watched on as
swollen late Spring streams of Heard such
tempos scrambled over easy unbuttered
whole untoasted wheat harvested by pre
maturely deliberate cockt Lobes of Listen
wholly fielding incidental ambuscades
accidently gleaned Calls respondable-ized
evaporably quicklied as these hours pass

slate, or check . . .

first off, we are faced with a blank slate : we'd not know
where such poems are came from, nor knew we don't know
where such poems headed. Or perhaps it's a blank check :
the wealth of its origins unknowned, plus we knew not how far
we'll get to go — will this poem even pay its own way ?? Will we,
picking up where we came in, end up bounced back into the Void...
is the poem leaving itself, or is it staying within itself — are such
poems headed from self deeper into self, or are they headed
out from self further than the self . . . how do we tell one
way or the other, or are there actually even always many,
many "other" possibilities ?? is sheer query all we knew,
know, or hold onto, in the beginning and/or evermore ?
And when we finally put such poems aside, where will
we be.. whate'er will've changed ?

consc, as a rule . . .

there are roles we intercede as we roll thru
grooves on out every way we can imagine not
withstanding that lack of assertively & definitively
maintained Humility the spectacle of a man avoiding
capture if you are or will become pregnant enough's
a congruesomely weaponized installed a cautionary
pre-actional firewall forestalling immediacy leaps
of mind/body arcs of sparky faith in outcomes
I've went & got old frail forgetful & self consc
ious not what I meant to say nor as well as I'd
meant to say it it's what the true pros amongst
us always do deliver the goods top-selfishly em
barrassment's four-square so's I embarrass myself
even when all alone when all's been taken from me

the daily dime . . .

without a net's nastiest iteration
precludes placatething wherewithals
of no known Yet just because I recall
it well doesn't mean which heir'd
whirled or'll take liberties believe it
or not we're not going back in's its own
cul d'innured depends with Her there was
e'er that sense of a spectrum of possibilities
where high protein impeachments rendered
repeatedly at speed occur'd there was a quality
of the tactical undeniably but this entails
emspirited bafflement at each examined
turn we deliberatedly took just in time to've
gotten enough of it down to go on Song'd

was where & All . . .

it delighted her that my sweet nothings were
that tirelessly complicated I do like my work but
hardly expect anyone else to said its umbrella'd
reign of error ringing wrought-eyed widely (decoy
duck on alligator lake behind the Waffle House)
that inordinate affection for inanimate oddments
time to do some serious birthing of the megillah
(far down the left side of the Peninsula nigh)
a slow thoughtful waltz sort of blues steady
Mama came a-tollin' sort of blues that washes
rather than weeps nor cries out nor refuses to
do biddings other than toll in taut clearly we've
been placed in an impossible situation wee
threadlets tumbling quickly emptful nowly

dread to Mind . . .

set up an anchorage &/or a raft upon which to
stand & deliver from the swoll River & was yet
sonic slave to the Poem its music slave to me
forms of somber & elegant oral scrimshaw known
was one but didn't yet know what one was poets
make words & words make worlds as well as Song're
what I knew fairly early on my consciousness a fish
native to & still needful of the deliberated Release
daily in those open waters yet only getting that
kind of work-out occasionally in spaced times at
best of late say twice a month on average what
specific kind of fish you'll ask well that's an apt
query the shark springs dread to mind as well
the whale of course & threads of frailest Gold

instinct anew

Back then I didn't know how to swim inside
it or even that immersion was what would
become the locus of my mobility. It wasn't
that the listening to was what mattered,
nay, rather it was listening as irreducible
navigational modality – wherever I was
headed, I couldn't get there without it.
Listening taught me not only what to
avoid, but what to embrace as well &
what was well worth noting en passant.
Being mobile wasn't enough – I also had to
recall that sense of notability... to build
the instinctive anew would require senses
I was only beginning to realize even existed

or is nor

there was an ugly incompletitude about the way
he'd shaped himself that'd belaid the sustain
how did you come by that degree of certitude-
cloaked discernment-sped dismiss &/or accept
she has 5 loves in her life her 2 puppies her
son her daughter & me in no particular order
stuttered in traffic connecting Ohio to Florida
I'm an amateur & what that means is that re
petition just ain't my thing or is nor does any
one in my resound expect any the less any
more than having been likewised even so
much as merrily matters whole lifetimes re-
gathered whole-handed brevities applied re-
troactive in extremis as Time itself recurs

tote that poke

I am of the tribe that leaves at this specific hour
Time's how we're identified our Time this one, ours
how you break a line & where you place a comma
I consider him a mentor tho' I'm as yet untutored
He is a citizen of his own worldview wherein
he hath convened a coterie of bolstering com
paneros look I am a primitive & well-unschooled
homily-beatified I need help but am not going to
get any's how it's pretty much always been you'll've
no doubt heard all this before'd you been listening
not having enough aural outlets meant meandering
unmercifedly recidivitalized where She goes his
consort steeply crypt-kept ungendered as opposed
to non-bindle bereft my poke's where we tote it, ja ?

thru free at . . .

retroactive in extremis & the Now as being
the Eternal are the held-to polarities we of
Memory's many progeny 'mongst bardic
barrenkind find as swung-within Groove
the very kith Harm's Way has as generative
bespoke Indeterminacy how each line gives
berth to each succeeding & giving birth to
how ear cocks & fires whate'er's writ upon
the winds of briefest exhorted vocal illus
ions come risen soundfully multi-dimens
ional in deed upon the instants that segue
on-stagedly where we of the ilk wend un
beknownst yet indelibly evaporate who
was manatee ilk broke thru free at last

. . . and only'll

maybe we're all just turning into mutants
just now I've always been an advocate of
immersion & collage from even before even
knowing such possibilities even existed till
Monk & Mingus & Bill Evans were ever what
I saw/heard that re-fitted everything already
not known I yet knew this very poem here in
front of you yourself's about you doing it itself
even as these words spill along beneath your very
scan this here's a flick about you watching this flick
but not so's you'd even notice 'cause you don't's
the whole point till you do which is da kine you
get or you don't get but if you do's like an echo pre
ceding the report truly recalled again & once only'd

happy/snappy (at The Brass Rail

the pendulu happy works its craft back & forth betwixt
paying attention & being snappily distracted where i sit
at table, back booth'd beneath my two walled poems
aye laddie, ever-poised to slip back into the familiar
chaos of gender-specified hyper-reactivity don't y'know
... well, what have I learned is that taking the slip-back
personally is a vertiginous error -- & that familiar throb
we feel ? take it as some kind of uncanny booster shot,
the stuporous-seeming after-effects of which will pass
down into the Primal Vortex, if only you have the Grace
to Sing beneath your breath while the breathless storm
passes on by quite the same as those jukebox lullabies
do, the ones that take my foot to rhythmic high alert,
recalling poetries simultane, hith & yon & coast t'coa ..

year's eve Ak-chronic

I'm just a guy trying to stay alert trying
to stay alive was its own sort of boast
no fount of askew folk filigree nor
jimmied deft whimple-mask blather I'm
the cat's gloved claw dealing one-handed
shuffles & toting up menu odds in belly be
damned grave greasy spoons down boule
vards of jokey hoke where decapitated
old hotels teeter vaguely in sun's slow re
verence for drafty vast echo-cathedrals
slumped across from cross-wired union
stations danced & breath-baked without
a care in the world anymore for select
stillborn stilettos of corporate shuck

nap time . . . ?

when we sneak away & become
dreamworld saturated such fabulous
Beings we turn into & it's as if the only
way we could keep from floating off
Forever is that we still have to tend
to our bodies' ills their more earth
bound functions if we weren't our
selves still animals in simple comp
lex fact we'd've ended up dining on
cloud, having sleighted ourselves
into the actual Angels our spider &
octopus disguises kept us from em
bracing when birds called to us just
this morning, just before the Dawn

Stolen Moments

Annie & Colin be-Cuyahoga River'd in Kent

Waning in the Wildernein
(chassis Sabbatica, Part Dos…

thence'd querulings

how to make poetry that begs forth a multi dimensional
Unknown that keeps looking back at you, as you
keep coming, earfully eager to resolve the latest
compositional modality - flywheel patterns that
seemingly pirouette mid-air, and nuts to le mot juste ?
Indeed, and in the throes of composing, how to do
impending line breaks, palpably felt before they
actually occur -- which word, or word partial, next?
Specifically enough, how many possible words,
that'll make the impend not just a drama but also
momentum's Swerve into unanticipated Furtherings ?

Deciding mustneeds wreak sprung unexpectancies . . .

ritmo/chateau's simulacra

wherever mine ear looks it hears a different vision
here a different Monk, there a different Bud Powell,
some other George Cables, Kirk Lightsey, or McCoy
not a matter of right or wrong but of majority's rule
spoke at once out of many mouths multiple shining
sirens ritmo-chateau'd the way some movie theaters
yawn darkly nearly empty media's a barking spider
masked or not smoking not standing or not sitting
we'll march come may past April shown yester'd
as if As If itself lingered loiterously, dallying near
duplicitously how the tongue simultaneously
forks non-stop the babble at the behest & sole
unsurvivaling bearded unbearably bygone over
lapping inexhaustibly brief stage-drops, dropped

Fomentasia

to read with a comprehending appetite
feels like flirtation & we know that won't
last now will it hysteria's murdering turn &
the placards thereof raucous after dark's
come undone as the new normal across
the Land closeted intelligence nakedly
near at hand as a land-line insistently
remaindering the reminderers never to
expect solvency solutions nor calmly
measured ripostes leveled so casually
behind whoever got there fomentastic
to the max like notable ne'er-do-wells
who grew gravely splayed explanators
loitering thirsty & lonely as poems do

auditing apprenticeships, shaped

needless to say hearing's not just what ears do they
make way like I'd like to think I'm telling you things you'll
never hear anywhere else a place nearby like none
other that's gotten to's an overheard snuck up upon only
everybody very suddenly could have heard as much if when
that made-way got landed on we'd known it for what it
watched & wondered-on listening from under which
side-longingly luxuriant shafts of brittle bravura cordons
snapping to & fro feckless & fancy free bells ringingly
gotten past the early day's hour or so penned handedly did
the poem have a silhouette &or undersides as well and
exceptions there were many at each memor-actualized
turn of a poem's eventuality availed intricacies boded
bodily as any other shade dancing aloud doth doeth

heading, for the head

aye such Kali lept slow lang syne dusk-glow'd slough
of pond-skewed gloaming-launched skiffs royale barques
de swivel that courtiers swive-allor'd till tacitly tremored
banks slip'ry slide first thought best thought form as
never more than an extension of one merest perception
applaudedly till toasted 'neath starshine balladry waves
loosely serenaded tipsy-washed ashore off the near node
immediately & directly leading to a further each following
each so that the leading sounded syllable composed in
the sequence of the musical phrase so revision after such
adamant provisos taken as being some other beast than
wit was overrated as was intellection intuition & muses
poetry the very beast that hides in plain earshot in the
after-worded resonance of the quickened whole

winter/midst

to have been assigned a portion slice or angle of
the pluroma that wafts ever Winter-midst of late's
no near mystifiably'd azimuthal arc-arrayed as
announced nouning of the nuanced ineffable thereby
not merrily mobile nor merely portable but wholly
because before you can trust the process you have
to create one which is it will be repeated Memory's
cue a note fluttering cluefully fragile & sound-sighted
the news that's immediately prior to whatever stays
and/or's fit to imprint upon airily Time's panic'd &
waveral addenda deep-ending widely without tho'
no more held to account than any other unremorseful
omen omni-overly speedy for that's the condition &'s
why we've gathered said yet'd's plaints & share them

echo dalliance

we've been on different planets for quite some time now
there is a planet of music & a planet of making music
planets of making & planets of doing & of slowing down
the planet of composing regulates input & justifies
the planet of collage introduces & juxtaposedlies
the planet of array invites borders to be crossed
& each visited planet hungers for us to stay there or
then again there's the laser pointillism'd Zukovsky guy
how troubling the clutter of obscurity becomes when
one's specific gravity goes all shrunken headed or
despised at best tho' typically somewhat unresponded to
it's how so much appears on Gotham's transpon oyster
so play wee houred synco ivory furloughs sloughed as
painstaken purviews flex, fostered debts of tune

not exactly None'd

he said the place he'd rather be was in between
the covers of a book after if it was good enough it's
a mystery's part of what you want this leading to that
shuffled vocabular arcane genuflected to inflections
gnotty nearly nonesuch was the con well-savored in advance
upt half incalculable tho' only so's you'd near quickly have
noticed on the way to one bye to summarily indigestible
but blamely blithe not at all the more autonomic tapped
wholeavened & recandescent was the ordure waftish
to be precis-lessfully apportionate Time out of Mind
here a ruined postal outlet there an anti-infrafracture
our lapsed decades of seriously racist inevitable &
ongone & greatly festered circumscription armed &
withered whether plundappled or tamped who's to say

Saidness'd

state of the art sleuthish matters as does breadthful inform
& the regalist distances thereby aura-accrued each one's
a distant rigging of the rhyth-wry's possible orders
everybody wants their own mesa of flat spun flywheels
played like congas minimum three an altar of sounding
we are in the realm of triads teeming 'round Time's panic
our theatre of verbiage arrays itself tympanically
these are not metric measures they're drum-amongs
sung sprungs consorting fork-tonguedly restless as if
it could have been such an impossibly lovely planet
if you found that of interest you might find this that
as well tho' otherly by all means yoked if only by
being similarly keyed in timely sequencing aligned
not by the said but by said's saying all in All

ne'er do swells

there are no wrong words in a poem only if that's how it's intentionally adjudibaited such was where we were coming from there to why knotted deliberate pitched bearing seized decks dancing duly levered in retrospun spiraling onwards recollected in whirlwound & ever-widening gyres o' patch worked wily but eludal, surely evadal as well we wouldn't credit a single syllable sans initial urgencies subtly savored predelectably anticipadoral you know the kind's right here before yr very scan pre-echo'g & there to be dipped unto and we do how could we not it's who we've always been mourners at the mirrored respond utterly stupefied but not so's retrospecious made-work mattered in the slight sleights tested flavoracious if at all fated without favor of a kind of tease the kind tempered but no less fond of

star-boiled Temperance

but I don't know what his situation is I understand
he's got a place downtown but does he have access
to a car even after all it's pandemic Winter in the City
these times are troubly & unforgiving in unanticipated
ways my son's removed himself to Batavia & even my
daughter calls in from FLA at best once a week or so
well at least they sang for Linda at the Echo last week
& tonight it's in the wee 30s with lots of squalling rains
but come New Year's it'll be edging towards a balmy 60
& years from now you'll be able to look all this up if
looking up anymore is still on our agendas we who'd
still be awake at such an hour in a broken star-turn
delivered by masked hand on the front stoop just in
time to receive a tract of sprungs fell-foldedly so

Will-dothic

rattling around within syllabic variables refusing
to kowtow to the intended cosmo-gratuaccessible
shapeliness left hither along the mustneeds as
care-packs reminder prods & nudges perhaps
the sounded syllabic reality shuffle hardly counts
as a Heritage now does it but it's what I've been
assigned the Mercy of Light baggage so as not to
have to pretend into the recessive embrace of what
the Void keeps proposing the thing about the Moon
is that it will not blind you nor burn you to a crisp
you can speak with the watch Moon as your ear &
you shiver because upon reflection whatever's mo'
bettah than that's still there above the rainclouds
sailing roundly syllabic as the poet did & doeth

state sleighted slovenish

look it's a different world already you should've No'd
how obviously goes the fit off-cock'd the leery shame
of hind-legged shameless heaving of extinguished chance
since those towers downed that blew Rudy's fragile taut
fracas-bent proclivitas careering wantonly but not so's
the polity'd even noticed the ice cubes in his ears
the melting wax beneath a nation's self-regard for
bows-no-longer nor rationed nor agenda'd they'd
sooner impeach their own appendages if only they'd
not long since accomplished nothing less than they'd
everlastfully dropped the doppel gung-ho of so
self-justaflexibly con-collusively continuing to
uphold interchangeable oppositive stampedualitied
coins of their debauchery nightsticks' drumbling

poise as If

whether I'm careful or careless's sorely bestride
that never known what possesses a man to publish
a book like short life housing Ravenous Diamonds
or this treadmill in hand which the doctor prescribed
much the same's he'd done so to so many of the others
all of whom alike to el moi look there are an awful lot
of really smart people out there who just don't know
how to plug in what can you say about what them
that they thought through their thrills thrown then
so many who knew so much without knowing much
more than that there's less to most of it than we'd
surmised back then nobody knew or even guessed
they couldn't get heard without or even with whether
or if you'd been able to retract any of else than they'd

in from on high

their survival depended on affection given & warmth
not speed which was why the rabbit always got often
away & why getting caught there was the new distant
downtown not being a neighborhood meant backyards
& the automobile gave the lie celebrating peculiarity
was beside points of disorder & hybridal fusions got
heard as accents giving account of was what we all
did then as now over-looming narratives notwithstood
my language was all translated thru '60s jazz from
a native tongue spring-loaded betwixt Vincent Gene
Richard Little Washington Dina Charles Ray Dylan
Bob Simone Nina & a veritable gumbo of Moreso &
none of it not nearly as non-neighborly as Gotham
when I got there from Akron tongue-tied ears open

stability too's a con

there is a multiplicity of forms & approaches
that approaches daily thru yonder gloaming
that gleams variously once nightfall flouts
at once merry & somber the wane sun grants
itself all regal & squint-bright till who'd've
held harrowings in the moonlit silencio gript
without chagrin's best-laid springtime sap
hapless unintended oblively rootsbound in
surrection ramified bent-banner bashed po
licemen's lives tattooo'd or otherwise well you
know how it is when you've a friend you simply
forgive him his patheticisms some beams'll stun
ja but others are more gracious & wait to make
the bench so much more welcoming come balm

Memory's the poet's secret sauce :
News that stays news that's always changing

whether or not a given poet acknowledges both mutability
and instability as crucial but not hard-wired derives rather
directly from keeping the Memory sauce utterly fluid Mom's
milk sours at room temperature — not to be nursed by fixating
on ideal controls is a kind of jazz poets of not wholly Grecian
formulas trust implicitly stepping off from apron strings that
no longer apply's where ear replaces the taste buds &'s where
the unwritten announces the scholar's demise where mama
loshen ends up being translated to actual poetry said actual
poetry's a rarity immediately apparent If I read a book and
it makes my whole body so cold no fire can ever warm me
I know that is poetry If I feel physically that the top of mine
head were taken off I know that's poetry said her then as
said sauce came to call quelling disputation liken'd to

mercy blinked

stumbling upon a generative modus's where it begins
I recalled having no true instinct whatever for avoiding
showers of fundamental compositional conversion rather
most likely a matter of an overwhelmed lust to just re
fashioned & make or break become rhyth-embarked up
on sheer subtlety in its least visited intimate environs
rendered vulnerable to mortal malleabilitized sup
pression's muted alarums as my language organellia
rose readied to be Else'd a kind of no holds barred
acceptance of remediated wordrapt sensivisitation
brought full-figuratively to bear repeatedly a kind
ness both overdue & exploratory yet unmercifully
recuriosing not knowing whence whither or while
line by line turned over & outrageously prancéd

even step by step's hard

longevity-wise speaking nearer to Beyond but no
not at all irretrievably so able to be back-brought
from clayed snares by touch prompts that defied
each due subsiding into who knew resistance was
the gift received rather than imposed a conscious
levy regaling lightly definitive not just by re-de
fusing disconnects made bridged briefly but oh
so commandingly thus Forever'd it seemed we'd
been named anew just so long as our depoise de
pended on being disputed and/or disrupted with
all due mem'ryless rebirthailing quick stroked &
almost as pens of attention hearded re-imprinted
hosannahs to nodded out glows driven cumulative
ly grandiose clues at Her roving boldly so triggered

doppel negativa

it can be so good to hold a single obsess thru changes
mostly moderated thru thoroughly while aided no less
minutiae'd via exquisitiae even if all you have left to show
for its gladly aesthetic exhaustion posing as just another
evening being ravished with ongoing horizons lowered
indistinguishably from uplifted who knew or really ever
needed to know more than that it could've replenished
itself openly & without reservation as descending glory
came strictly focused on multiplicities of wee surprisals
yesterday's already a lifetime ago, and no, each remaining
day's forth-shadowing is never not more harrowing than
tomorrow's blind allegiance to whatever's come prior to
what's carried all thru every hour's minute to minute in
tractable progressions for better nor non anti-erudition

thus, continuanced

my face was a creative entity able to impart as She
came to know lately beneath such clutter as mustneeds
be both shelved & routed withal such partnerings as
took/given simultane that way we lovers always due
leaving each arrival riding's leanings bequeathed to
ongoing's eternities of focusings thus'd in rushes of
our blent & mixt playful yet intensely re-purposed as
Elsa for instance who wanted to do it right but then it got
out of hand erudition turned into perditious reminderings
that some of the smartest people we knew are thick-eared
the clutteryings were no excuse tho' She never allowed such
proclaiming verisimilisound-rescued from oblivion how can
it even be but anything less than even more perdition but
here we are nonetheless busy anywhere you bet stayed

Strictly then-Some'd

GOOGIE'S BAR

As a late teen newly removed to Gotham from Akros, I went to school on the multitudinous enjambed argots of the City, sitting, ears acutely cocked and tongue wholly abeyanced, entranced as often as I could be in that thenced-festering all a-yap Village watering hole. Somebody referred to somebody else as taking "the needle in the neck" and I was a goner . . .

pre-POSTSCRIPTURAL
(notes, noted amidst y whilst)

"There is a transcendental
dimension beyond language -- it's just
hard as hell to talk about it."
- Terence McKenna

Talk about's a defunct methodology &'s been that all
along. TMK's calling attention to the Ineffable Zone,
the border of which is the place the best poetry takes
us right to the edge of, & yea, such poetry does so at a
speed that imparts an irresistible momentum - we are
tipped into that Dimension with startling ease, having
been utterly shorn of normative balance.

The shame of poetry is that the loss of said Specific
Unbalance follows so quickly. Almost before the first
echo fades, we are upright once again, our crock-lit
solid footing once again cocky with unremembering.

And the vanity of the written word is that such
paradoxical echo-awakened Instability can be
contained. Well, only the bones of the Beast can be
kept in the print museum. Its breath & blood are
namore, just that quick.

Transcendence itself's both exceedingly temporary &
abruptly transitory . . . the Quick, and the Gone.

Nature of the Beast.

yea, Robert

can't say I've ever knowingly heard
coyotes howl, but I've sensed the
presence of that wolf known as
honor & fame nipping at Norman's
hide ("he's a fool who'd strive to
swive her") ... as for the gods, I see
them at happy hour in my local,
loitering & barking smoke in
profile whilst the jukebox bawls
with rhythmic monotony, them,
at their ease, tippling idly, on a
late afternoon break from their
grander rounds... wouldst we,
you and I, join them briefly, eh ?

biding, bye the bye

what was the best thing 'bout that room ?
long about 4 or so, more ladies than gents

& I do mean Ladies, typically in their 40s
or 50s, which won't work for me anyway

near as I can tell they pretty much talk to
each other & as for me ? I talk to myself

not out loud I save that for the stage
up all night most nights – still talkin' &

uncommonly good at hiding in plain
sight -- listenin' now ... who does that ?

Bar None, just t'other day

*-a la Norwood's own
Rick Isaac, on bass*

it wasn't just his tone it was the clarity of it &
the charity in that clarity being so neighborly
yet so much of it a staged terror masked w/
inconsequential visual noodling derivationally
smuggled in on the sly while the Great Real World
happened nonethelessedly you maybe its witness
if only so many pressing distractions weren't so
risibly omni-apparent you probably didn't know
he's my cousin's Dad you've gotta be kidding on
the Eve of the 4th of July clearing the clutter from
the field upon which the dancing will occur yes
he used to be a musician each one's a tendril of
the Divine & every syllable's just one note shy
of the Melody supposedly rippling ever onward

Darrel sails away . . .

They serve & too they die howsoever
good or ill they may or might not've
ever done they were our daily Theres
there on the good days as well as the dull
on the slow ones the silent & the loud
crowded game days & torrential rains
of snow & ice & garbage pick-up days
days the kids never call nor do you &
when you brought yr dog along & days
you shared memories & the crossword
shared yr take-out's fine dining theirs
& yours & bought a round you tipped
or forgot to having drowned yr tipple
till came Time's Close, ever & anon ..

still the same old story

I Heard it in the Echo
the Echo heard it, too
this the only thing we
still really love to do…

some come here from afar
others from near, taste
buds all at the ready,
big ears ready, too...

Echo so faint, Echo so loud :
laughter from back o' the House
elders flirt, too, up along our bar
even gossip from nearby booths

if you ain't been here lately
bet your ears are hungry, too
our ears & tongues so busy --
BOTH all up in the Echo stew

You, too, bye the bye, will hear us
in the Echo, oh You will, so don't
just chew & savor our chatty din
by all means, pilgrim -- Enter in !

KEVIN, at the Rail

No, Kevin never got to sail the Seven
Seas the way, in his youth, our bartender
Darrel did — our Kevin had football on his
his mind but his body betrayed him . . .

our K was a smartphone sailor, sitting at
the bar by the hour with head bowed
until he heard one of us say something
careless, which always caught his ear . . .

Kevin the Quick, Kevin the Knowing,
veteran of the construction trades, who
could put things together & take them
apart -- he advised us all, free of charge

yes, Kevin was quicker'n you
not much'd get past him even
after he slipped & fell & ended
up crutch-bound he'd lean 'em

against the bar & his pal Eric used
them that day as props when he
did his Frankenstein Dance while
K was lost in his phone on the bar

Kevin had about a month to live
after Eric danced that way then but
who knew that - Trifle didn't nor did
Otis or any of the rest of us not at all

Eric found him & nobody got to
stand & speak at the funeral but
they still tell tales at the Rail &
we all still watch for his red truck

we all heard that abrupt way he'd
say whatever he had to say often
times funny always to the point
big man K rarely wasted his words

we Hear him still & always will
& see him slow walk into the bar
the memory hurts & always will our
K, a citizen of these parts forever More

She owned one

we lived in old hotels downtown
with bars nearby so that harsh
raspy warm tone of voice of hers
was on a deep level in me
                old home familiar

I was pre-disposed to like her,
& I did, right off – her name was
Tara & years ago she
                owned one of those bars

Till the Time : *till* it

so ah'm anotha fuckt tomato
          but ah'm sayin' it out loud
the reason he can't sound off
               off the top's

y'hear things different when
          they're writ upon a page
the blood & breath o' memories-made
ain't in him, he's hot to be imprinted
& print's become his grave

it's all about me & nobody else this
world's in a twist what won't
be missed was what I am
          & am still am

the trick ? slay or be slain, stay
alert / stay alive   till y'die

what we do

smokers are smokey blokes :

not everybody's normal – me ?
my ears are funny nor do I not
wander off inside at times

I like what She likes another
cherished chink... well
there you are

the man's making it up
it's what Makars do
after All

came in nightly

old guy toddling 'round, nobody to tell
him his zipper's down I've been
drinking beer & smoking for
better'n 60 years, no way
I'm gonna stop now

Franny talked tortured & no, was no kind
of dancer so whatever made her walk off
kilter garbled her tongue, too ... her quiff
tasted of powder & well... that's just
who Franny really was

no, big Mama, I don't do
that anymore less'n you're
special & yeah you're
that but, see

we're all Gods until
we're not's just
how it is

The River and Lake Erie

No city fronting Lake Erie's breadth has quite the
moxie of fated Cleveland, what with how its crooked
River hath journeyed south, west, and thence to the
north thru Poetry's North Eastern Ohio barrens...
when the River at last conjoins with the Lake, there
within sight of downtown, the Poetry of its traverse
bubbles to the surface just offshore, eerie echoes that
the poets of that town take as their birthright : the
River rose vague thru farmland, thickened thru tyro-
runic Kent, then bounced west thru high Akros, till it
finally stole & burned Its way up into Cleveland :

  our U-shaped Wonder that is the Cuyahoga,
    collector of Prophecy & Song,
        Cleveland's uncanny necklace,
              strewn upon the damaged Plain

APPENDIX

some familial correspondence

some commentary

various asides

What I want the Appendix to do is give just enough "suggestive" insight to allow the reader connect the dots, mostly on their own — tricky, but do-able is my goal. Subtle, but tasty : In the same way that the collages appear sans explanatory accompaniment, so those Appendix entries — I will tinker with them to get them a bit more user friendly, but I'm not going to give the reader a narrative to account for them... they are correspondence entries and they are a furthering of the poet's field of reference, his back-up array sampled as indications that the book's evolution sprang from a sense of community rather than from isolationist visionary oddity. And I want to trust my involved reader to catch my drift as to why those entries are process-inclusive . . . emphasis on "process."

We can't go on. We go on. Certain interlocutorial guardrails loom oddly, unexpected and wholly necessary … if only just, but principally to, remind us. Herewith, a notably limited few that, personally, have kept that faith :

my band, Sasemble, at York St International, Newport KY 2001;

top row, from left: James Quilligan guitar & harmonica / Ralph La Charity, congas & poetry / Anne Marie, saxophone
bottom, from left: Mickey Morgan, dancer / Dicky Williams, guitar & light percussion / Jack Walker, sax, flute, light percussion

Pegasus above the Ancients

The Kawaji Correspondance

Six years hence, what follows is a kept correspondence from Ken Kawaji, he who once was a downtown Cinci Mr Fixit & Factotum, as well the resident events & readings programmer extraordinaire, there at Kaldi's Coffeehouse on Main Street in Cincinnati's Over the Rhine neighborhood (too, there are patrons at the Harvard bookstore in Cambridge who still recall when Kenny was an uncannily adept & astute cleric-of-all-seasonings, there) ... aye, Kenny, you did such good work over the years in the olde Cinci neighborhood, so changed & so utterly the same when you return for a walk-thru now & then – so yes, this bygone letter will be followed by your more recent missive, the both of them much better understood just by my having typed up each of them for this book heretofore in hand which I now will send to you in tardy respond . . .
Here following, some correspondence from Kenny since he moved to the Boston area :

Year of the Dog of the Earth

2018 ce

Spring and the dandelion clock

Dear Ralph, the years ago I walked far and out from a letter that started with another letter that begins with a wooden horse title that burned all gone now to forever by twelve years of the fire cycle and that turns yet again to quench in the earth.
Friendly fire you've said. Written. Aloud and

allowed. Yes, I've received the Litanies. Grateful to be remembered and thought of. A gracious and rare sending. Thank you and my apologies for waiting such a long time to sot out my desk to find a moment amongst too many excuses to write easily of such a fine book to have close at hand.

Songs. Sang, see sung and strum, seen sun saw summed swing summoned.... And still....

To the confession of my crimes, I refer to the philosopher's elixir that's used up all the good words. What are the OEM parts left over since God sang bhang; the winding stellar engines, the unnamed artifacts, the vocal prosthetics ?

And if the best poem can be made in the throat, this is because the throat is the midpoint between the heart and the brain. The poem is a thing which cannot exist elsewhere than in the head of the poet. It isn't beautiful out of nostalgia, it isn't beautiful because we recall some thing seen which were beautiful, nor because it describes beautiful things that we have the possibility of seeing. It is beautiful in itself and it doesn't admit of terms of comparison. It cannot be conceived anywhere but in a book. In summation, I find that the young poets with their secret recipes for making poems have the air of carnival barkers. They stand at the doors of their dives, screeching at the passersby : "Step right up ladies and gentlemen, right this way to poetry unveiled ! Come one, come all ! Here everyone is a poet ! Step inside and write your own stanzas.

*In my view, we must strive to bring about the birth of
a poetry which has never existed; to grow in our field,
not in that of our neighbor, nor on the planet Mars,
this precious planet which we lack and for which we
are searching with such anguish and avidity.*
-Vincent Huidobro

I know that you are sensitive to commendation and
compliment. So, I'll say just the last that, and leave be.

Still, the Litanies hold both ideas that Huidobro speaks
of; the voice and the book for all twelve quartered
and full restless winds yet reads as a narrative whole
different in each sitting, each setting. You are the only
poet I know that fills unbridled all such that is there:
*…and in poetry, beauty is no ornament: it is the
meaning. It is the truth. We have that on good
authority.*   -Ursua K. LeGuin

I have a great affection for the voice in/of Aralee Felt
Strange. Southern tomes of Dancin' in the Wake.
After reading through the Litanies a dozen odd books
went to the poetry/paper recyclers. Things kept
though; long ago in a magazine called Soaptown,
issue #3, 1989 – Aralee's, the 1st time I read it :

The people speak
*a bird in the bush is worth a
bird brain loose in the land
the land worth two in the world
the world in the bush bird hand
worth two bird brain loose in
the world bird brain loose*

who cares who's running things

and I convened a moment over another favorite cahier,
A Little Bastard Book for Buddha, by Major Ragain :

.... And hear the Heart Sutra,
without hinderance,
in my jawbone.

We'll sing 'til the wandering souls are found, while the
suns fill the song of morning,   we'll sing 'till the
bells they sound, and ring the bells of rhymney 'til they
ring inside our heads forever...

And remembering Mike M. all those nights sorting out
what from whatever in a basement full of books with
a jazz club over our heads and Xavier basketball on the
radio. My first year there I catalogued his collection
of records and moved thousands of books from John
Coleman's Acres of Books to Kaldi's basement.

On a poet's headstone in a western field some words
I heard are struck, and I remember (perhaps not well)
their shape, a dandelion
Come Lord Wind, strike me and I will fill the meadows!
-Richard Wilbur

Worst of all:
Not to die in the summer
When everything is bright,
And the earth is easy on the spade
                              -Gottfried Benn

I work alone here the most part trying to find a space to shape. I don't write much but take notes, make notes covered in reference and inference as is my habit. There are libraries here and bookstores and I come and go when I can. At the Harvard bookstore the manager Mark, who remembers me, says that anytime I come in and if any of the booksellers can name me then I get the employee discount. I remember listening to Geoffrey Hill read from The Triumph of Love in a rare book library room at Harvard. There were fine, old books in magnificent cabinets surrounded in an ocean of woolen carpets and medieval illuminated upholstery. The light was a bowl of coronation yarrow in a shadowed mass of wine red curtains that pooled on the floor and hung far upwards like a ruffled collar in the crown molding. Thickened back held the summer sun out and hushed all the concrete. The audience listened raptly to the poet in black and the audience of poets watched each other listening. There's an interesting bookstore out in Montague Mass, The Book Mill on the Sawmill river. Books you don't need in a place you can't find !

Me dearest Barbara and Zuzu the brindled cat has rendered what has been difficult for me as easy as I've ever recalled. So, I've gotten a little lazy being so well loved. All the things that once could barely fill a hip pocket have grown into more attachments than I can easily sort from recall. Still I'm busier than I prefer. I have a small private practice with an office in North Cambridge and one in Central Square. I do occasional work for Harvard University Wellness and I have an outcall hospice practice. So as a bodyworker my hands are now concerned with the shape of the house of the spirit. It's muscle and sinew, bone and tendon, organ, skin and fascia and all the myriad variations from 23 pairs of chromosomes, eight arrows of chaos, 64 hexagrams, the stations of the cross, sutras and salahs, the glamour of wearing the years of the common era and its long before and yet to be. Taut line and tension, mainstays and spinnakers, foot weary from landing and running and aloft the rhomboid and serratus crease the heavy line where wings once hung and so much that's wary of the world is strung lace weary and hums its cause and cure :

Pray
Bowing to booming sermons
pray with the lowing herds
that on the day of deafening
we'll be too wise for words.
-Morgan Gibson

I have no complaints.   My respect dear friend   -KK

(and here following the most recent of Ken Kawaji's letters :

26 Nove Ember, year of the Dragon
Ralph,
Here's the Péguy book I said I would send. I left some reading markers in it for no reason; it's intact from the last time I read it. Others have marked it, too. It's a small book. It is outdated and perhaps outlandish in point of view, point of fact.

Strange relevancies abound, though – similarities in time and tenor. Some parts can be read as stern and unyielding in tone.

I've included a local piece. Poetry ? Well, I don't know anymore – too many influences grace the lack of discipline, the autodidact's stubbornness, and friendlessness in the general intellectual topiary – the bohemian conceit. Still, it's what I do for what it's worth. Most of my audience nowadays are captives of my stationery.

Best of this season of spirits to you and yours   KK

(Nota bene : as for KK's regard for poet/filmmaker Aralee Strange, yes – she was and remains much revered here in Cincinnati – note scholar/poet Tyrone Williams' review of a Dos Madres book's memorial tribute for Aralee by yours truly : https://jacket2.org/commentary/farewell-and-all and now, here following, Kenny's above alluded-to bohemian conceit –

"Poetry?" …. Beware :
Trophies of the Deadland

By Ken Kawaji (Nov 2024)
Today is chore day, Tuesday I am feeling
Like Tyr, ever the god of war, who also cleans the
kitchen does laundry,   mops,
and sweeps. Dishes must be done before or
after eating while I grind   my

teeth on a dream swallow that wears down
the canines in pursuit of an end to chew.

On that morning, when the night guard gets stuck on
protecting my teeth from protesting
that war, freely speaking, sucks But clean thinking
scrubs the book of law
decorated with dread, drear queer things, dead so
dead that what my mind inherited from listening
earthwards to the dirt, says
my ears hear whatever I have (a brain. I'm smart),
you see.   I
vacuum out my hair, which is evident
when I dusted off the lottery ticket, I found there.
What a steal.   Probably, just
a flower wins it all anyway, and I get lost again

In the end.

Kombucha made, coffee grounds out, cleaned the litter
too, then lunch in lostness   until dinner, and in the
groove from my sleep last night, the sound of a little
round   dream callous from a fiddle found
living on the thumb of a rose.

Pricked on such music was my
graced-up, bingo-burst life. The
cognitive   slovenly far fucked dumb
keister-busted
  knuckleduster of a movie whereby,
a sinister character
        and a zillion zany minions

die namelessly. Still, the world
survives   this bullshit enough
     for a handful of zeros
    to row to heaven in a little slow boat.

Thus, the chorus, the cliché –
the patient humble inherit
          the thimble of the earth. A worm circles
the middle of nowhere. Ouroboros
the parasite that swallows itself. A thread of things
that unbinds   when yet is
finished. A trip that's all bumps and no speed. Time

and Ginger helps with the dizziness when we are
traveling together or   we're done
for the day.

It's not a lullaby or a theme; three gods in darkness lie –
Woden the Father, Thor,   and I. This trinity of
whim. Am I wrong ? Who sings this song

of songs on a stormy morn, what a mess sometimes
(the grandee lord gentlemen He)   only appears to be
dead, dear me. Once slumbering and now awake, the
day   crashed, and he cries. Let fray my shoddy
armor once more, as always. Away, away,   away until
Father's Day. It's always Wednesday, with or without
you, he says.

I start over again because he's the king of the dead, the
god of the wind who blows   today away, and on
the threat of thunder, what is Thursday, my brother for
tomorrow, bound to say ? That I cleaned house that
I'm here to stay.

120

And finally this, a further find from Kenny, from more than a decade ago :

Ken Kawaji responds to FAREWELLIA :
May 17, 2014

So odd for me to be caught up in this latter career, and so busy from the vantage point of being sixty. I'm sorry for not having been in touch earlier after you did me the honor of sending me a copy of Farewellia.
The event of the book, bard death and live memory. It's been overwhelming and my thoughts have not been all my own making, and I remember, but those too are often framed by the other.

My long walk on deck from Cairo to Pittsburgh shaped in a square watch, six on then six off and six on and six off and so on seven days a week, the Ohio river through the lens of the after watch. One night I watched a poet deck hand dive off the hurricane deck of the boat, in the Oxbow bends, swim ashore. He said later he left a poem at every mile marker from Paducah to Cincinnati. Everything I know is there. My lover here? I met at Arnold's. Same as cycling Steve Lansky poet laureate of Over the Rhine. Back then.

Aralee I first knew as Etta Stone, heard in a 6th street basement of a Japanese steakhouse rented from a Christian cudgel of a man, Mr.Brendamour. And you and she...the first view from Crazy Ladies. She started and you ambushed and I was startled to see, to hear such a thing. I remember the long length of her gaze, the resonance of your pace. A grace there and space. It would be much later that I understood, in a small way, the complexity of that respect.

Here in the north I stay quiet, work with my hands. Stay temper, stay brag, bray of remembrance. Who knows? Less care. Up here. There's no dismay even yet. My mind is still bright with delusion, hallucination, and as a matter of fact; changes always. Thinks right and left with, no other than otherwise thinks that too.

Some years ago my sense of smell, and taste were also left to memory. The physicians weave their hands in an incantatory shrug, idiopathic et al. Though you told me once, over a turkey meatloaf, that you remember what things taste like, that your seasoning is tempered by experience of the memory. I cook that way now and answer the same question in much the same way.

I was reading Stanford's, The Light the Dead See By, in the beginning of this Year of the Horse. The Chinese moon calendar told in a Bukowski title: The Days run Away like Wild Horses over the Hills.   Don't they just?

Zendoze more ancient yet

(NB : the reference is to FAREWELLIA a la Aralee, from Dos Madres Press 2014 . . .

Multi-year Facebook dialogue between poet/scholar Tyrone Williams & Ralph La Charity; excerpts begin in 2012, extending up till Tyrone's death in 2024:

Our correspondence began with my calling Tyrone's attention to an erroneous notation in one (he had more than one Facebook nom do guerre!) of his Facebook bio notes . . .

Tyrone, 9/8/2012 > my error--when I was typing in "Central High School" I mistakenly hit the first entry that surfaced--Manila Central H.S.! You wouldn't believe how difficult it was to delete it and change it to Central High School, Detroit, Michigan...

Ralph responds > gee, for a while there you had an exotic past, unbeknownst even to yourself... how many others, not just me, thought so. by the way, myself and a six year old girlfriend used to set fires in the alley behind the Belvedere Hotel next door to old Cass Tech High back in Detroit in the late '40s (she and me were the harbingers of a pyro-tradition aborning up thereabouts), but you'll never see THAT tidbit on my F'bk entry.... one just never knows, eh ?

Tyrone > didn't know you were from Detroit!

Ralph > I was born in Bethlehem PA, but we moved to Detroit right after the end of WW2, I would have been pushing 3 I guess... Dad got an office job in the

Penobscot building and we lived in the Belvedere...
when I wasn't torching with my sweetie I'd be up on
the hotel roof, staring at smokestacks, or be out on the
sidewalk looking over the shoulders of Cass Tech art
students... I can't recall where I did 1st grade, but by 2nd
grade we'd moved to Zanesville OH for the rest of my
grade school years. You get to hear all this because you
DIDN'T go to high school in Manila ! So — when's your
next reading ??

Ralph, 9/2/2013 > Sunday, September 15, at the
Northside Tavern in Cinci, a tribute to recently passed
multi-talent Aralee Strange --- I might have already
sent you an invite via the Aralee Memorial page on
Facebook a couple of weeks ago... should be both a
moving and overdue recognition-type get-together --
Did you know her very well ? you going ??

Tyrone responds > will try... thanks for letting me
know... I did not, I met her through my late colleague
Lynda Hart and, in general, through the reading series
around town (York St, Grammer's, etc.). We knew each
other well enough, nodding acquaintances, but sort of
drifted apart even before she moved to Athens GA...

Ralph > one of the things they'll do that night is show
a video montage of her in her later years, down there in
Georgia... with regard to the poetry impresario part of
her engagements, I always perceived her as being one
committed to listening in & thereby learning about...
she wasn't pushing a program so much as finding out
what was willing to announce itself. By the time she
got down to Georgia, that poetry impresario factor

124

had become strategic to the point that she functioned very much as a guide to possibilities theretofore uninvestigated -- she took advantage of a scene that didn't even know it was poised to Become. She brought a level of experience to bear on what she initiated, and was quite successful in helping the poetry scene in Athens, Georgia wake up to itself. She made an interracial, all-ages, all-levels kind of poetry scene possible there... and it happened, at least for the term of her involvement before she passed. Difficult to say what will become of the flowering she abetted, but for a few years there, it cooked.

That Tyrone found my poetry of interest first came to my attention via this review :
https://www.poetryfoundation.org/harriet-books/2013/10/oracular-redux-the-poetry-of-robert-murphy-and-ralph-la-charity
Nota bene / I never did send the following letter to Tyrone – instead, we became occasional breakfast &/ or lunchmates, friends en passant, as the following journey in part documents :

Hey/hey, Tyrone !
(10/30/2013,)
I was touched by your words, re Robert Murphy and myself… such a surprise !

Back when I first went public as a poet, in the late '60s, the modus was hand-to-hand, which pretty much is how it has stayed. Long about the mid-'70s, following Ed Sanders lead in his INVESTIGATIVE POETRY template, we took seriously (some of us !) his notion of keeping dossiers of each other's work &etc in our private files... that too is pretty much how it has stayed. This then is the spirit of what I'm sending over to you --- hand-to-hand, as background for your private files.

These are a few print versions of what I do. Seatticus Knight was my last book-length project, from a very long almost 30 years ago... it is soul-depleting to put oneself thru a project like Seatticus, only to have it disappear, leaving nary a trace, which was what happened : the publication date was delayed by its printer a couple of times, Linda and I moved to Europe shortly after the book eventually came out, and that was that. The two chapbooks are fairly recent – I have just found it so much more convenient and inexpensive, over the years since Seatticus, to simply run off such bespoke copies, for friends and such... the computer makes this efficiency possible, and the consequent hands-on distribution to individual known contacts is way more satisfying.

Also find two archival copies of the Seattle dollar mag, Open Sky, from the mid-'80s (when Seatticus was being done)... Sky was a quarterly volunteer sort of staple-zine, each issue appearing in a run of four hundred copies --- to get published in Sky, what you had to do was show up on collating night with four hundred copies of whatever you wanted to have included in the new issue... well, what me and my collagraffitiators did was show up with four hundred ORIGINALS, each original consisting of a single 8 $\frac{1}{2}$ X 11 sheet containing an original printed poem by me interwoven upon an original visual by of one two artists I was then working with, Aholaah Arzah & Michael McCafferty --- the pages were each unique, each page a coming together of two creative spirits. Our discipline in making the pages was to do them at a rate of five a day, without pause till the number 400 was achieved – then, in they all went on collating night, an ambush by us on the whole concept of a magazine composed of "copies." We were so pleased with ourselves that we did the whole discipline once again two issues later, coming up with another series of 400 originals.

So --- those two bouts of original collaboration yielded a total of 800 original pieces, which 800 simply disappeared into the Open Sky project as a whole… the two copies of Sky herein each contain one of those 800, which you can find therein by going thru each issue carefully. Originals. In a dollar mag.

When push came to shove, I was personally dissatisfied with having our work disappear that way, which dissatisfaction was transformed into the book, Seatticus Knight : Having kept photos of what we did, it was a matter of my going back thru them, and from that trove finding and making the book. Voila !

Finally herein, find an archival copy of W'ORCs/Aloud Allowed, which samizdat I began publishing from Europe in the '80s, then from San Antonio for a few years, and finally, from here in Cinci till it gave up the ghost in 2006 after over ninety issues.   It was in W'ORCs that I'd begun making my own collages.

Ralph 3/24/2018 > well, lunch at Eli's was grand, sure helped get me back from FLA - - thanks for how it all worked out. Here's the listing for that Jake Berry review I mentioned : " Poet/musician Jake Berry of Florence, Alabama, takes on the whole of Ralph La Charity's Litanies Said Handedly, in long-time Australian arts activist & editor Mark Young's OTOLITHS online "magazine of many e-things" ... https://the-otolith.blogspot.com.au/2017/o6/jake-berry.html

Tyrone, 3/27/18 > thanks for the link....I emailed Andrew of Chicago Review but no response as yet... from Andrew Peart at Chicago Review (first communique in seven months)… I took the last line as the most promising part of this email. I'd already started rewriting the first two or three paragraphs, disentangling it from the Morris book and correcting the factual errors. Guess it depends now on the other editors.: "Hi Tyrone, I wanted to write quickly to confirm receipt with you of the three reviews for the special issue—the Harris, Martin, and Holiday reviews. I'm meeting with the CR gang this week to firm up the production timeline for the issue, and I'll write back after that with a clearer sense of the timeline for edits on the review. I'll also bring up the very welcome suggestion of the Ralph La Charity review and see if Eric Powell and Geronimo Cruz would like to take the opportunity to see it into publication. The book definitely caught my attention when it came out."

Tyrone's 4/3/18 addendum > CR turned down the idea because, though defunct, The Constant Critic webpage is still up. The editor said if the site went black before year's end they would still be interested.

Ralph responds > yeah, makes sense, I get it - CR is only protecting its own critical brand. Without a do-over that is essentially divorced from CC, a new review rather than a cleaned-up version of the CC review, why would CR have wanted to touch it ? And yeah, that damning website being left up, dangling like a foreclosure that has no conclusive end date... foreclosure forestalled in perpetuity, but ever-threatening, by a first draft's unkillable existence, eh ? This has become a further wrinkle to the old conundrum -- no longer "damned if you do, damned if you don't" but now "damned no matter what you do, damned no matter what you DON't do" ! A new review that touches on the old review only in the sense that the old review was an earlier approach to reviewing the poet in question, in the same way the Harriet and the Jacket reviews were earlier approaches, is the only viable answer . . . there are several things in that old version that are really worthy of salvaging & developing, but the new review would have to be not a version of the old, but an evolution beyond the old. Probably should have seen this one coming . . .

Ty, 4/3/18 > i think the initial interest--on the very busy Andrew's part--was genuine and due to his reading past my "corrected version" phrase in this original email, but truth to tell, i really think they would have gone for it had not TCC been still live (Eric's email opened up with "I see The Constant Critic is still live...").. I am indeed thinking of COMPLETELY rewriting--and thus divorcing--the new version from the old version and thinking about Plume which just ran

my review of two more coupled books. Joshua Corey,
ironically also in Chicago), DID give me a chance to
correct errors, typos, etc. so Plume is my next venue...

Ralph goes on > ever Onward — how it was, is, &
will be . . . Plume will be the new target, oyez. And
one of the angles I noticed in that old CC review that
could be cleaned up is the polarity biz betwixt the
oral & the written. It seems to me that one of the
basic demonstrations the LITANIES makes is that a
dichotomy comprising those two approaches need not
be highlighted, if the given book can show the two
aspects not only co-existing, but actively "colluding"
— the one feeds the other, coming and going over the
course of many years And of course that other thing,
more personal to the reviewer in this case : You were
actually there the night all the poems in the book were
delivered, aloud and in the exact same sequence as
the book's sequence replicates, those 60 poems, off
the top... and the whole of that evening's deliveries
were delivered both non-stop AND from memory,
Poet-memory, that particular emphasis on memory
being one of this poet's insisted-upon foundational
bottom lines. A third angle that needs addressing is
the matter of fame/notoriety, as conflated with any
desire on the poet's part to actively court an audience
per se -- I stayed in the shadows of the open reading
presentational near-anonymity for so many decades
because to me a poet's work is not only resonant in the
moment but it is also ephemeral in that same moment
-- "written on the wind" is a condition of open reading
praxis, and LITANIES is nothing if not an overview,
retrospective celebration of Open. The loneliness of the

long distance practitioner comes to fruition in the book
. . . maybe !

Ty's next day response > true, but per oral/written
issue I was trying/was going to/point to those issues in
their reception modes--readings and publishing--but of
course never got a chance to get there...

Ralph responds > yeah, you got a major screwing
behind them printing your draft rather than your
final/final... fascinating that you are thinking along
reception modes -- in LITANIES, reception is not taken
into consideration. What the book tries to highlight,
specifically in its extra-poetry commentary (the
preliminary comments in the front of the book, the
intro comments that lead each poetry section, and
of course those two appendix entries) is the poet's
own sense of what he is doing. The extra-poetry stuff
is an attempt to get into the point of view of the
author, and is meant to address, however obliquely,
the paradox that is the problem of authorial intention
vs audience/reader reception. The Wizard lives in a
different flow of intention than the Wizardines -- there
is comedy in that paradox, and the varied commentary
additives play with said paradox. There is precious
little that is unintended about how those extras
address the fact of the poetry's central mysterium
: maybe these poems work, maybe they don't, but
here are some clues that might hedge the bet. If a
given artist's intent is not known somehow, there
isn't much chance a judgement upon it will be useful
-- my sense of LITANIES is that, as a whole, it is a very
deliberate project. How do the back-of-the-book links

to performance vids work for you ? Their inclusion is
not a form of self-advertisement -- they are there to
give further ballast to the book being a very deliberate
four-square attempt to peek behind the veil of what
this poet is, and has been, up to.

Ty continues > I think ballast is the right word, the
interweaving of sound, film and print, very much
akin to Morris' book...so, yes, I was thinking about
what you weren't, the problem of reception not only
among critics but also specific audiences (that's why
the acknowledgments of the bars and coffeehouses
are crucial for my thinking about those audiences vs.
traditional poetry reading audiences in academic/art
gallery/etc. settings).

Ralph responds > Again, how the poet views what he
is doing versus how an audience reacts to that doing
can be worlds apart. I usually wouldn't have negative
experiences when I stood & delivered in public,
although it did become apparent that there was a sense
among some of the other poets that my performative
elan was a bit much, competition-wise, with "How do
you follow THAT?" being a frequent reaction. Another
aspect of my preference for open readings is that very
thing -- the presence of other poets who are also an
active part of the overall reading dynamic. Still another
factor about open readings is that they are woefully
under-appreciated, even by their participants -- there
is a bell curve continuum at work that isn't always
apparent among the participants : open readings are
cumulative affairs that have at their disposal more than
just one poet after the other, standing there reading

only what they came intending to read. No, there is a
far-end, high protein end to the curve, where the best
& most fertile open readings occur -- in such readings,
the gulf between audience & readers gets messed with
because there is not much difference between the two
... not only do the two poles intersect/interweave,
but all the best open readings have more than one
round on offer -- the cumulative final effect has to
do with poets reacting to what they've been hearing
from other poets – it's that perdurable call & response
element, always threatening to make its appearance at
an open reading. An open reading encodes possibilities
that are expansive rather than restrictive. So that one
comes away from the best open readings knowing
that one has unfinished business in that particular
cauldron -- the open reading is, typically, open-ended.
There are echoes & challenges that get carried away
from the event. An appetite for Further is what
an open reading offers that the traditional poetry
reading, composed as it is overwhelmingly of audience
members, cannot match : Reception is marginalized
in favor of Reaction, the one being somewhat passive
and inscrutably non-reactive, the other being actively
heedless of reception to the point of being practically
confrontative. Granted, that many open readings do
not get to the point of dynamic interweave between
participants, which is usually the result of bad hosting
-- unless an open reading includes more than one go-
around, ya can't get there from here. As well, there is
a statute of limitations for poets like me : eventually,
after several decades, the search for the ideal open
poetry arena beggars the prospects -- I got tired.
LITANIES, therefore, exists also as a farewellia -- the

book is a history of my engagement within an arena I no longer have the personal gumption to pursue. I'm an old-timer. The book tells what I used to do.
The other aspect of the book, the one that seems to be the most elusive in your critical response, is the presence of those twelve color collages. Maybe you'd just as soon prefer to skip attempting to account for their presence, eh ? Fair enough, but they are the unadmitted "rest of the story" -- they are the dynamics of an open reading told in the shapes of what occurs to the poet INTERNALLY while standing & delivering ... they are pictoral embodiments of the kinds of occluded mental fireworks that go off while reciting. They are not visual poems -- they are visual echoes of what the act of reciting occasioned within the mental hologram-in-extremis of the poet's Doing ... they are in flagrante delicto of the recitational poet at work.

Ty's response > yeah, the collages I enjoyed but I took them as more or less visual 'analogues" to the poetics under the poems--the interweaving of disparate but related elements into a temporary "whole," but as you can tell from this exchange--already longer than most book reviews--the other consideration is how much space you can get in a publication. I know I told you before but I am still puzzled by the constraints on word limits for online publications. Clearly it's not a question of space; it has to do with assumptions about the attention-span of audiences. I mean, they may be right (I grew up on books, not IM or texts) but it's still frustrating.

Ralph's next day respo, 4/5/18 > Helluva thing, for sure... what does not change is the will to change is how Olson put it -- not sure he had any notion of YOUR dilemma tho' ! The assumptions you are up against, what a crock to have to deal with. But whether or not you do a compact, shortie review (a la the Harriets) or a longish one shouldn't constrain your effort anyway, the point being if the book itself is adjudged by you to be worth the trouble, you just go for it, wherever your own inspiration takes you. As for the book's visuals, my talking about those collages was not meant to guide you so much as get what you just gave me... a sense of how you accounted for them, and what you say is cool -- "analogues to the poetics" is definitely a way to say it that honors the spirit... my own take was more a matter of my own sense of the book's attempt to get in behind poet-mind & reveal stuff about the poet's own inner experience while doing the public work. The other thought I just had was, hey -- if you're doing a bottoms-up re-write of the review, maybe that would pass muster for a reconsider by Chicago Review ... just a thought.

Did you take a look at that Jake Berry review yet? Maybe reading some other reviewer at this time would just interfere with things, but his take was pretty touching, personally -- he got it in a way that allowed for enthusiasm as well as bright insight, so hey, it was NOT a lukewarm response.

Ty's continuance > Yeah, I like the Berry review. I think CR is out as long as the CC site is live...what I'm thinking is doing something like Berry did, a profile-ish thing.....also occurs to me that our dialogue right here in this space might also constitute the kind of

discussion CR, jacket 2 or even Raintaxi might be into...
https://www.dispatchespoetrywars.com/commentary/
a-review-of-ralph-la-charity-litanies-said-handedly-
poetry-collage-performance-by-tyrone-williams/

Ralph's > Yes — maybe a profile with a dialogue
addendum could work... I like it, you bet. Berry review
did a dialogue addendum, too. Then again, your notion
of our current dialogue isolated/tweaked to be used as
the centerpiece of a discussion-centric submission has
great appeal - To do something that BEGINs with the
dialogue, and then segues into a profile -- that would be
a nice reversal, eh ? I await your Furtherings . . .
And YES ! -- your renderings last evening at the
Mercantile were superb, particularly the warrior orisha
litany.. and that flowers piece wasn't bad, either..
alongside Rothenberg's sound poetry renditions, they
made the event trebly memorable for me -- thank you !

Ra's, 1/19/2019 > Heavy duty sashay of yrs thru
BWatten's criticality in J2 -- a big WOW to You !
Ty responds >   and as Barrett notes, I only surveyed
the outside...My original ambition was to do a long
article/essay on both The Constructivist Moment
and Questions of Poetics...the review is, finally, an
unsatisfactory gesture in that direction…
Ra's > jeez, Tyrone -- I have to admit that I've merely
"surveyed the outside" of YOUR piece ! but yeah, I
fully understand that reaction you're having... tho' I
don't do much that would be considered criticism, the
sense that I could have done better is always with me,
no matter the genre etc... dissatisfaction reigns !

Ra's, 2/16/20 > Linda and I are down here in FLA till the end of March, so I'll miss the fireworks impending at the Lou-Con... I see where you're weighing in alongside the estimable Mr Watten -- what's THAT all about ! ? terrible way for your school year to end... even worse for Norman, what with retirement and all, helluva way to have to say adios, eh ? I had no idea about your own unstable contretemps vis a vis Xavier... as for the Echo, early in the day would work, say 8:30 or so ? not that I've noticed them being crowded yet at any hour, but mornings there have not looked to be well-attended at all... a definite maybe if you want to try it. Tyrone, you told me once of a memorial sculpture for Black soldiers that's downtown and that you had a hand in - what's the name & location of that piece again ?? I thought you'd published a booklet referring to it all, but I can't locate the booklet. Any info you can post my way would be greatly appreciated ...

Ty's respo > Smale Park, the Black Brigade tribute, kitty corner to the stadium facing the river--I wrote some of the text and "poems"...

Ra's, 1/16/22 > Aye, Ty -- have you any idea how red tide boring South FLA can be at this particular time of year, snowbirds long gone, rainy season not here yet, nothing but "Now Hiring" signs everywhere ? Looking forward to getting back North around the end of June... you be available for some lunch long about then ??

So sorry to learn your Day of Days is marred by your having self-maimed on a recent dog-walk... would it help if I got us pulled pork from our usual meet-up spot down by the river ?

Ty's respo > Thanks Ralph, but probably not as my appetite has also been affected by the whole experience (knee-braces to prevent bending knees for 6-8 weeks, a constant state of wooziness due to drugs, etc.). Rather wait until I can actually enjoy eating again, mid-March perhaps...

Ty weighs in, 2/19/22 > yes--thanks for asking...I still rely on the walker when I go outside to get the mail or drive a bit (I've only been inside the post office and a vacuum cleaner store so far) but don't use it a lot inside the house, relaying on banisters for the stairs and counters and tables to move around inside...Just started outpatient physical therapy this week. The knee braces come off this coming Wednesday but I've been warned I may actually have more trouble initially getting around. Still, I'll be happy to be braces-free...Hope you are doing well.

Ra's goes on > thanks for the update, Ty... I'm sure it's been no kind of fun as the weeks stretch on... but you'll get there. I've been trying to wrap up my latest book, but motivation seems to be a problem... the final shaping of the project shouldn't be this amorphously tepid, but that's the way it's shaking out -- you finding any way to exercise the other parts of your being ?? Gaining weight would seem to be something that might be an accompanying problem, too . . . is it ?

Ty > yes, not so much in the hospital but at home, with cardio exercises permitted, the weight gain is becoming an issue...another reason to look forward to the braces coming off, which will mean limited things like the stationary bike...sorry to hear you seem to have reached an impasses in the manuscript.. I actually think that's not uncommon an experience (along with the inner whispers of doubt, uncertainty, etc.). Presuming there's no immediate pressing deadline I am sure you will get pass the moment...

Ra > yep -- sometimes, the braces are wholly mental, so it seems... had all my lower teeth extracted two months ago, on the way to getting a denture eventually, and that's probably a contributing factor -- altered articulation dilemmas, body image instability, not being able to bite into stuff... quelle drag, all of it. Being cool & conscious of the difficulties doesn't lessen their impact, eh ? Sorry to lay this off on you . . . grumpy jive from Ralph -- just what you needed to hear, eh ? We WILL get thru it, and thank you Jesus for the no deadline thing. You're handling your online classes with elan, I trust ... ?

Ty > yep, the sudden shift to remote worked for the students who have been nice about that...however they are anxious for me to make my semester debut in person (mid-March, maybe)..my brother in law had his teeth removed and is now in that waiting period before he can get implants...and he is, according to my sister in law, in misery...

p.s.--I sent you a request to use your statement about preferring poems to do rather than be, a nice Olson-esque touch. I'm working on a short essay on poet Lloyd Addison and that's exactly what his poem, "Umbra," seems to be enacting...he's making it do...

Ra's reply > I suppose it's also a Spicer thing-- wanting a real lemon as the meat of the splay, so to speak... the poem as its own Grandpa, too, to get all down-home about it, eh ? I look forward to reading the essay... I'll be researching Umbra & Addison — not familiar with it . . . thanks for this all :

The near-constant de-recontextualizing of grammatical/syntactical/denotational expectancies, word by word & line by line... the umbra as radiant black hole regurgitating all but Praise for the Lady ? The seven pages of Lloyd Addison's stirring poem tasks all but the most forgiving of perdurable endurances. Given that such cleansing confusions are our Age's prerequired discipline now as in his time, I am finding that, since you brought it to my attention, his "umbra" keeps pulling me back in, and each re-reading brings me closer to its Whole . . . thanks for the heads-up. How's your piece on his piece coming along ? I'll be back in Cinci for a few weeks right after April Fool's Day – you ambulatory enough yet for a visit to our favorite pulled pork bistro long about then ??

Ty's > still in initial stages of gathering more materials--not a lot of it--on Umbra and Addison...glad you keep coming back, are being pulled back to, the poem.. going to try to teach on campus next week so that will be a test...left leg still not strong enough to go without a brace but I've migrated from the walker to a cane so that's good...

Ra goes on > Your gathering of more materials is crucial -- at this point, the poem itself is my sole evidence... it would seem that you are on the case leading to something as yet unprecedented, so that I can only salute the effort and await the findings. Meanwhile, for me at least, back thru the gravity of what is there as this mazing chapbook, its witness, its function, its desperation & its insistence... o ! the agony it limns, the exaltation it so twistfully insists upon . . .

Ty's respo > Found out yesterday the MRI revealed another tear in the left knee so surgery tomorrow morning, which means I won't be able to meet next Wednesday...another six weeks in that knee brace...

Ra's > scheiße ... not quite as bad as what you're going thru, but I've been without any lower teeth for a couple months now, in prep for an eventual lower denture, and yesterday, seeing as how one thing always leads to another, had to have a root canal done... who knows what the future holds, eh? If you need a reader for the Addison paper, count me in -- I've got the original chapbook now, too... was looking forward to letting you take a gander... oh well. just caught up to some of what Aldon Lynn Neilsen has to say about Addison... also, that Neilsen and you did some performative collaboration... how's your Addison paper coming along ??

Ty's, 5/11/22 > I'm afraid the essay strays far from your comment but at least you get a seat up front... "Umbra," Umbra and the Society of Umbra (Ty's copied essay follows : "I prefer the poem do things rather than be about things. To play music with someone, for instance, means you get to know them in an additional way – not necessarily better, but certainly additional, which is to say you know them on another plane than the intuitive one, or the occasional one, or the accidental one, or the survivaling one . . . and it's very intimate, too. And that intimacy matters. It's why ! prefer poems do. Be about's nowheres near that mysterious."   -Ralph La Charity

Cincinnati poet Ralph La Charity's FB comment about poetry and music manages to elude the conventional horns of the modernist poet's dilemma. Should a poem foreground meaning, a position usually ascribed to the so-called "low" modernism of Sandburg, Hughes and other working-class poets? Or should the poem, in Archibald MacLeish's famous quip, "...not mean/ But be"? La Charity prefers otherwise, noting his preference for poems that "do." La Charity addresses both the performative facet of poetry—long a concern of his— as well as the social character of reading poetry while accompanied by a musician. La Charity's ideas about returning poetry to its oracular and musical origins are not new; poets have been performing with musicians as long as poetry has existed, though the rise of the poem and, in the West, its hegemony as a written document has meant that its oracular and/or musical function has had to be insisted on, sometimes polemically, at various points throughout Western history. So accustomed have we become to the poem as a written document that, in the United States at least, these moments of recuperation have been understood as innovative interventions. Thus, we had the Beats and The Last Poets, for example, and since then we have had a variety of oral- and music-based movements generally categorized as Performance Poetry. However, what is emphasized in La Charity's brief remarks, and all too often underemphasized in discussions of poetry and poetics, is the social aspect and effects of oracular- and music-based poetry. As our demystifying literary histories remind us, social formations have been an important, even decisive, factor in the promotion, distribution and apotheosis of the page-based poem. Still, La Charity's comment on the unique social relation formed when, say, a poet performs with a musician, a connection, he insists, so intimate it cannot be reduced to intuition, occasion, accident or survivaling, bespeaks a mystery unfathomable by the McLeish poem that simply is.

I want to pursue the relation between social intimacy and para-aesthetic mystery by way of the Society of Umbra, a loose organization of black poets, painters and musicians (1962-1963), its magazine, Umbra (1963-1974) and the Lloyd Addison poem, "Umbra," (1961-1962) that gave the group its name. Although organized as a cadre of artists, many of its members were driven, to various degrees, by domestic and international Pan-African political and cultural concerns. These three manifestations of umbra— as poem, magazine and artist collective—arguably capture, or attempted to capture, La Charity's "social"

categories—intuition, occasion, accident, survivaling—
insofar as they presuppose relationships to others.
Nevertheless, La Charity insists that none of these
relationships are as intimate as that "mysterious"
one between two performers (in this case, a poet
and a musician), elevating a certain kind of aesthetic
experience above and beyond the social. Aside from the
written memoirs by several members of the Society,
we have no way to approach the intimate 'mystery'
of what might have happened during performances
(readings, music performances, or some combination
of both) during those weekly Umbra workshops.
However, the very term itself—umbra—may capture
something of that intimate mystery La Charity invokes,
one that might bring us closer to what those workshop
sessions may have been like for its participants. Though
my primary focus will be on umbra as it functions
in Addison's poem of the same name, I first want
to invoke another term, "aura," that appears in the
title and throughout another Addison poem, "By line
abdomen cradle aura womb." This poem immediately
follows "Umbra" in The aura & the umbra, Addison's
1970 chapbook. Inasmuch as both poems concern, in
part, the black female body, the aura and umbra may
well embody—if that can even be said about such
terms—something akin to the intimate mystery La
Charity invokes in his remarks.

(nota bene – Tyrone's Umbra article-in-development
continues, here following's 6 page insert – as of the
publication of my book in hand, this review by Tyrone
has not been elsewhere published) :
However, along with an aesthetic experience evoked

by words and music (e.g., the opening lines of "Umbra"), Addison's poems also distribute black female body parts in a field of linguistic particles and particulars that deconstruct dialectics in general. Mystery here is existential, not just aesthetic. But pace the labyrinthine paths that mystery, aesthetic or existential, may lead us on, I begin with a question that is less a mystery than an inquiry. What if the artist collective had chosen to name itself the Society of Aura? On the one hand, Lloyd Addison began composing the poem, "By line abdomen cradle aura womb," in 1959, around the time Raymond Patterson and Calvin Hernton were organizing readings in and around the Lower East Side, but before the artist collective would coalesce around Patterson, Hernton and the remnants of the leftist political organization On Guard Committee for Freedom in 1961. (7-9) However, Addison would not complete "By line" until 1965, two years after the dissolution of the Society. On the other hand, his poem that inspired the group's name, "Umbra," was composed 1961-1962. We don't know when, or even if, Addison read "By line" to the fledgling collective. We don't know if the group was aware of the earlier poem, and even if it was aware of "By line," it may simply be that the group preferred the racial, cultural and, above all, social and political connotations of the word, if not the poem, "Umbra," to the cumbersome title of "By line." Though the two poems would not be published together until 1970 as part of the Paul Berman series, the title of the chapbook, The aura & the umbra, as well as the "arguments" of the poems themselves, suggest that Addison refused to valorize either aura or umbra as concepts. The ampersand in the chapbook's title, conjoining the two modes of emanation, makes that clear. At the same time what remains obscure, a different kind of mystery, is the nature of the opaque body that casts these two kinds of emanations. Or is it two degrees of emanation, suggesting two moments, two points, along a spectrum? The argument for two kinds of emanations, for essential differences between them, would note that an aura is usually understood as invisible while an umbra is visible, however amorphous its boundary. This argument might also add that whereas an aura is generally understood to emanate from a body, an umbra, as a shadow, requires a visible light source outside the body. The argument against essential differences, for degrees of difference, would note that both the aura and the umbra are dependent upon an opaque body from which they emanate. This dependency would imply that for both a material body is the precondition for their very existence. This point is at the heart of Benjamin's critique in "The Work of Art in the Age of Mechanical Reproduction" even though, for Benjamin, the aura is a supreme value emanating not only from the physical work of art but also from its inimitable temporal and spatial nexus. Benjamin never commented on it, but these same spatial-temporal constraints also apply to the umbra. And though he was willing to cast the aura of the unique work of art into the dustbin of history for the liberatory political possibilities implied by mechanical reproduction inherent to new genres of art (e.g., film), he did predict that the ethnocentrism implied by his concept of the aura would not only survive but would also multiply during the age of mechanical reproduction. It is in this context that the umbra comes to the fore as the other of the aura, duplicating the very problems that should have dwindled, if not disappeared, with the hegemony of the unique work of art.

What are these problems? Historically, the singularity of the unique work of art gives way to its mechanical, potentially unlimited, duplication, a sedimentation of techne that covers up—in the Heideggerian sense—its social and cultural origins, without which, per Benjamin, there is no aura. This is, of course, primarily a problem for those invested in preserving aesthetic (and perhaps class-based) hegemonies. It is, however, a potential problem for the insurgency of the other that extols the democratic ethos implicit in mechanical duplication and reproduction; this ethos is always at risk of converting into another kind of hegemony, e.g., the insurgent triumph, however symbolic, of the umbra over the opaque body of white supremacy. For example, Addison's poem, "Umbra," may appear, at moments, to stake its own hegemonic claims. Such a misreading would depend, however, on veiling the poem's aura, radiating "behind" or "outside" the poem grounded in its cultural and historical contexts. Under the regime or shadow of white supremacy—Jim Crow is alive and well in the 1950s and early 1960s— Addison executes a series of moves that confound the aura/umbra and, even more significant, body/ emanation distinctions delineated above. Here are the first two lines of the poem: "My sun has gone down in drum suite penumbra/ The mood of this rhythm my body is umbra" (8) Nothing may seem odder than the possessive that opens the poem, "My sun."

We can read this phrase as a pun if we recall that the first poem in the chapbook, "Carpentry," refers to the occupation of Jesus of Nazareth, the Christian prophet. The poem is a critique of religion as the congealing of spirituality ("wooden feeling") and the presumption of Christian revelation ("What do you mean man/ no one before knew the meaning of God?" (3)) But because the narrator of "Umbra" personalizes "sun" it may be that the first line is a general critique of the hegemony of the visual, even as it gives way to the aural. However, this is less the reversal of a hierarchy than its suspension—the sun goes "down in drum suite penumbra." The visual is literally marginalized, setting into the edge of an umbra, but it persists within the horizon of a field where darkness and shadow cannot be distinguished: "The umbral body is in penumbral field." (8) The "mood of the rhythm," its aura established by the 1957 recording of Drum Suite by Art Blakey and the Jazz Messengers, centers the body as both a darker object and nonobject, violating the law of noncontradiction. In the spectrum of darkness and shadow - umbra and penumbra- the body/emanation distinction disappears.

Or rather, and more accurately, one mode of the body/emanation vanishes. Is it possible that the aura survives its multiple replications, all those copies, for instance, of Drum Suite? Given its amorphous, indefinite nature, the aura, we speculate, survives just as long as the imperial mode of the first-person plural, for example, survives as the phantasmic residue—no longer a singular emanation—of a coterie, a cult of insiders. Displaced across time and space, "we" reflect, and so, confirm, the aura as a residue (as fans, not fanatics), however diminished, of mechanically reproduced artworks. For once the mechanically reproduced artwork and accompanying aura disseminate horizontally—no longer nailed like a stake into a singular historical ground—both can once again claim a kind of populist hegemony. But this claim cannot be reduced to mere numbers, the determinants of the popular and unpopular. On the contrary, the aura of an artwork subject to duplication struggles to overcome its dissemination, its reduction to mere residue, to claim a singular status as unique in spite of its multiplicity. In short, in the age of mechanical reproduction, the historical aura attempts to detach itself from the artwork on which it nonetheless depends. In this historical context---midcentury American culture, for example—the specter of the spectrum (e.g., the porous border between the popular and cultish) is determinate. For example, although the jazz album and book of poetry are both duplicated for their respective markets, there are fine distinctions between and within these subgenres of music and literature. In general, in the late Fifties, jazz sells better than poetry, and this commercial gap holds true for the smaller markets for avant-garde jazz vis-à-vis avant-garde poetry. One might conclude then that the poem in general, and the avant-garde poem in particular, has "less" of a struggle to retain its aura as a "unique" artwork than the avant-garde jazz album since, in this context, commercial "failure" is read by a coterie, a "we," as confirmation of the unique. Some jazz albums lay claim to their auras by attempting to arrest the evaluative consequences of mechanical reproduction by naming the dates and locations of their recordings. The illusion created by the singularity of a place and date on each album manufactured tempers (ideally) the adulteration allegedly inherent to mechanical reproduction. And whether it was Berman's or Addison's idea, The aura & the umbra attempts the same, though it doesn't go as far as some jazz recordings; each poem is followed by the year (but not location) of its composition. Insofar as the aura is, for Benjamin, a check on a runaway transcendentalism that would unmoor art from its historicity (call it bad idealism), the dating of poems without specifying the locations(s) of their composition takes a middle path between the determinants of specific locations and dates of composition and the indeterminants of "a midcentury" poem.

In the two Addison poems under consideration the "anchor" of a year or, in the case of "By line abdomen cradle aura womb," years (1959-1965) serves to prevent the drift into transcendental idealism. The overt subject of both poems -the body of a black female - also curtails the abstraction, though a critique of the opposition between the concrete and the abstract is also part of Addison's strategy. The "line" between the parts of a female torso—abdomen, womb—is physical, biological, while "cradle" and "womb" may be read as metonyms for childbirth and pregnancy even as the sequence of words in the poem's title reminds us that the abdomen literally "cradles" the "aura womb." As if to emphasize the primordial mystery of birth, the poem begins in a celebratory mood: "Thigh clay oh thigh clay is genius!" (15) In "Umbra" the thigh is also celebrated: ""just as yes is thigh flesh moral beautiful/ this address is a carriage itself for horizons' hills" (13). But while the thigh is one among several boy parts invoked in "Umbra" ("Her hair is lackluster," "her forehead is arched...," "her eyes seed..." and "her face is a slope..." all occur on p. 10), the hips, legs and torso are the primary body parts invoked in "By line" until the coda of the poem. Here, the aura takes on some of the mystery La Charity invokes, but instead of a bond between poet and musician we have, by implication, a bond between, potentially, a mother and child and/or male and female parents. The "aura" of that bond is ethnocentric only inasmuch as the child, like the unique artwork, has a known birthdate and birth location. In this context the undocumented orphan and illegal immigrant, whose "internal" and "external" threats to the integrity of the state are never singular (where there's one there are more), are equivalent to mechanically reproduced and forged artworks from the point of view of Culture. The threat of another, who is none other than the author ("To desert my love's space I left by volition/ cloudy-eyed Delores") is more pronounced in "By line abdomen cradle aura womb" than in "Umbra," yet the personal dimension of both poems and, most important, their celebration of the black female body hints at yet another question, The "carriage" of "address" in "Umbra" has been displaced; "Out of the swim the boat is distress" in "By line." Poetry has taken the place of the human body, a trope that takes us back, at the very least, to Shakespeare's "as long as men speak English..." by way of Wordsworth's "food for Future/ years." Was the decision to adopt the title of Addison's poem, ostensibly about the parts (especially the parts relating to sexuality and childbirth) of a black woman's body, a kind of compensation for a few black male artists with little interest in black women as intellectual, romantic or sexual partners?

In "Slightly Autobiographical: The Sixties on the Lower East Side," Rashidah Ismali-Abu-Bakr recalls her sense of isolation and the hostility she felt from some members of the Society of Umbra. Ismali-Abu-Bakt notes that in the heady atmosphere of the early Sixties, freedom seemed to mean, for some black men, interracial possibilities: "Bouyed [sp] by a historically more progressive and diverse zone, Black men ventured freer with their white female partners, arm in arm along the cluttered streets with fruit and vegetable sellers from Eastern Europe (although few would be so bold as to stroll after dark along Hudson Street or go too far south, into Little Italy)." An attendee at some of the early Umbra workshops, Ismali-Abu-Bakr began to notice a regular pattern: "After a few hours of discussion of the latest poems and the contents of so-and-so's novel the girlfriends would start to arrive. I had to leave early because of my son, and I remember having the feeling of being left out.

Somehow, it was after I got out on the street that I would notice that all of the women were White." (585) This apparently painful memory leads her to a wider discussion of the rising conflict between black woman and black men in the immediate post-civil rights era:

For me this was a painful time. I was separating from my husband for the first time. Alone, with a small boy, trying to complete graduate school and write, I felt very estranged at times from my ebon scribes and painters. They made it clear they were not interested in me because I was Black, African, and too ethnic; i.e., 'not beautiful.' Besides, I did not do drugs or drink. In fact, cigarette smoke made my eyes tear and my throat choke. To add fat to the fire, I had strong opinions and was extremely independent. These were the '60s, and Black men were coming into their own. Black women had to understand their manly needs, walk ten paces behind, submit to male authority. We were not to question a man's work, even if it were incorrect. We were to dress "African," assume the persona of "The Motherland," and raise little revolutionaries. Most of all, we were to remain unconditionally loyal to the Black man and never, under any circumstance, be seen in intimate association with a White man. This, of course, was in stark contrast to the behavior of almost all of the men I knew--excuse me, brothers--who had not a single "significant other" but several White women as lovers and wives. Calvin Hernton was to chronicle this dilemma in Sex and Race in America, and he was willing to tackle this sensitive issue in serious dialogue. (586)

The issue is not the accuracy or veracity of Ismali-Abu-Bakr's account. It is, after all, only "Slightly Autobiographical," a polemical gambit meant to establish a link between her personal experience and a broader cultural phenomenon. What is at stake om this context is how little black women appear—when they appear at all—in the memoirs and reminiscences of the black male members of Umbra. As I noted above, we have no way of knowing, of course, under what circumstances the collective was exposed to Addison's poem: at a reading, in a publication, in manuscript in a workshop, etc. And as I also noted, the original members, like Dent and Hernton, may have simply liked the word itself. Yet, if they did hear or read it, if they did have a general sense of its subject matter, the gap between, on the one hand, aesthetic appreciation and, on the other, personal choice, long with, if we can trust Ismali-Abu-Bakr's narrative, social behavior would be not unlike the distance between the poem and world under the lens of certain New Critics. Theoreticians of the poem as "being," not "doing," some New Critics emphasized the poem as object in order to ward off what they saw as sociological and didactic readings by critics with socialist and Marxist tendencies. Another way of saying this is that, for the New Critics, the "literary" might well be understood as dependent on its distance from the world. David Grundy notes that Umbra came into existence in part because Dent and Hernton, who had been involved with On Guard's political protests at the United Nations, wanted an organization "with a more literary orientation." (9) No doubt, given the different aesthetic tastes of the members involved, the "literary" probably meant different things to different writers. What is being emphasized here is that these differences aside, the underrepresentation of black women in the group and in the group members' personal lives is, at the least, ironic in relationship to the Addison poem that inspired the organization's name. It need hardly be added that irony was one of the principal tenets of the New Criticism.

Let's assume, however, that all this speculation is beside the point, that the group members chose umbra as its name because they felt the word spoke to their marginal position vis-à-vis mainstream American culture. Leaving aside the question of whether or not the collective ever heard any part of the poem "By line," one might still wonder if umbra was the best choice for the group's name. Might not this name imply that, in addition to the marginal position of the artists themselves, black culture—music, art, literature—is merely the "shadow" cast by a hegemonic white culture, a relationship quite different from one that situates black culture within that shadow? Might not this also imply that these artists were the cultural equivalents of E. Franklin Frazier's black bourgeoisie, black copies of white artists? Of course, if the "sun" of Western civilization seemed to be setting (exemplified by On Guard's protests at the UN, anticolonial resistance throughout the African continent, the growing popularity of black race records, etc.), then white culture (imagined as the aesthetic monuments of Western civilization) cast a shadow gradually elongated, and in the darkness of a night to come, or already arrived, there is, as noted above, neither object nor shadow to the naked eye. However, we know from a variety of memoirs by members of the Society that the group was disillusioned by, in Lorenzo Thomas's phrase, "literary New York" and many drifted back to their homes or to other cities across the nation, suggesting that "night" had yet to arrive, that white culture, epitomized by New York City, still maintained its hegemonic powers. While the rise of the Black Arts Movement in subsequent years was without question a significant, perhaps unprecedented, siege against white hegemony, it is not altogether clear that the white literary establishment was, in the end, eclipsed by the insurgents. To do justice to the history of the Society of Umbra and, more important, black culture, we would need to trace the subsequent developments of each artistic genre—jazz, painting, poetry, etc.—within the domains of music, art and literature to measure what is likely their uneven impacts on, generally, American culture. Even if we confine our concerns to the question of literature, we'd still have to ask if the black literary inroads into "literary New York," even if staged from outside the city, have finally overshadowed the tradition of white supremacy. This assessment is complicated by changes in technology and, specifically, delivery systems that have revamped, or perhaps marginalized as irrelevant, the very concept of the "literary," to say nothing of literature, as a stable concept, in general. If a "leveling" of the field of literature—e.g., the advent of Amazon as a delivery, publishing and review outlet, widespread desktop publishing ventures, the small press and magazine networks—reduces the literary to the status of an outmoded genre, attenuating its functions, however conceived (e.g., didactic, objective, etc.), such a demotion threatens less the anti-literary bohemianism of a Haki Madhubuti or Amiri Baraka than it does the black literariness of a Lorenzo Thomas or a Calvin Hernton. These issues underscore not only the different concepts of literature (and perhaps the literary) among the Society's members but also the different understandings of the relationship of literature to the political sphere. As David Grundy notes, the decision not to publish a Ray Durem poem about John F. Kennedy in the wake of his assassination (the poem was actually written two years earlier about the Bay of Pigs fiasco) in the group's magazine Umbra illuminates the "…broader and increasingly hostile arguments about Nationalism and integration within the bohemian, intercultural artistic communities of the Lower East Side."

The first two issues of Umbra reflected what Grundy calls the collective's "two main points of origin, one poetic and one political." (7) Thus, activists like the radical nationalist Robert F. Williams and future congressman Julian Bond were published alongside the experimental poet Oliver Pitcher and future novelist Patricia Brooks. In the three issues that were subsequently published, the magazine became more literary, featuring primarily "professional" writers of fiction (e.g., Ishmael Reed) and poetry (Julia Fields), though it continued to publish writings by musicians (e.g., Sun Ra) and painters (e.g., Joseph Johnson). Thus, despite a revolving and unstable editorial staff, internal dissent over content, persistent funding shortages and a haphazard publishing schedule, Umbra reflected the Society of Umbra 's commitment to sociality in the broadest senses of the term. Moreover, the extent to which the motives and intentions of many of its members remain shrouded in mystery only contributes to the aura that envelops the collective to the present day. Of course, all, or rather, most, literary magazines are social to the extent they are open to writers who occupy a certain bandwidth on the spectrum of literary aesthetics. And almost all little magazines endure a topsy-turvy career for any number of reasons before they finally cease publication. Thus, Umbra acquires its aura—in the non-Benjamin sense—for the same reasons any other number of little magazines from the Sixties and Seventies do: the subsequent career of those that appeared in the magazine. Historical significance being retrospective, it is not surprising that more and more critics are beginning to investigate and analyze origins and post-collective ramifications of the Society of Umbra, and thus, its members' individual and collective publications as the ripple effects of the Black Arts Movement begin to wane. It may be that in uncovering whatever "mystery" may be gleaned by reading the pieces published in the five issues of Umbra, readers may get a sense—but only a sense—of what it may have been like to be in attendance on those Friday nights in someone's apartment on the Lower East Side.

Works Cited

Addison, Lloyd. *The aura & the umbra*. London: Paul Berman Heritage Series, 1970.

Grundy, David. *Umbra* magazine (1963-1974): An Introduction and Bibliography. Among The Neighbors, 15. Buffalo, New York: The Poetry Collection of the University Libraries, University at Buffalo, The State University of New York, 2021.

Ismaili-Abu-Bakr, Rashidah. "Slightly Autobiographical: The 1960s on the Lower East Side." *African American Review, Vol. 27, No. 4* (Winter, 1993), pp. 585- 592.

La Charity, Ralph. I prefer the poem. Facebook: Posted February 19, 2022, 2:00 a.m. Retrieved Feb 20, 2022, 12:15 p.m.

Ra responds > oh yeah -- and I'm most intrigued by the social element you emphasize in the assay... I'd gotten to the point in my own speculative wonderment that I'd pretty much settled on the notion that the female element in Addison's umbra was in essence Mother Africa ... and yeah, the use you make of my comment was fetch-Furthered from my own original intent -- not that I'm complaining, but your take was more accompaniment-based, whereas my own sense was of a collaborative interweaving wherein poetry & music fuse to the point they become each other... Addison's poet-sensuality had a mystical radiation to it that the Umbra braintrust shied away from, eh ? How's your healing coming along - ? I'm looking forward to an in-person chat about what you're up to in the piece . . .

Ty's resp >   Right, because I wanted to emphasize the social rather than the aesthetic elements....it might be that the editors may want more of the latter, which means diving deeper into the two Addison poems. Problem is, essay is supposed to hit 4000 words. At present it's about 5000.....will know more after next Wednesday when we need I see the surgeon for the six week post op.....

Ra's > it is rather jargon-lingo laden there in the middle portion -- I could see cutting back on the more heavy-handed rhetoric in that section... I think what I am wrestling with is that 1,000 word over-the-limit aspect, and how to cut some things... I think where I started to get lost was in the "what are the problems" paragraph -- the Heidegger/Benjamin complexities thru me off, which may just be a my-own-limitations sort of caveat, eh ? Another possibility is to just jettison the parts of the piece that try to make use of my own quote, eh ?

Ty answers > Well. I'll wait for the editor's comments but I too think the Benjamin stuff may be too much a digression. But your quote is, for me, too crucial to jettison. Both editors took a quick scan and thought the piece was okay but they're waiting for other writers to turn in their essays. The book is on the Society of Umbra

Ra's > well, August 1st is almost here... maybe it's almost too late already, but then again word has reached me that you are still laid up -- I would love to drop by your place for a visit if at all possible... my curiosity about your Lloyd Addison paper-in-the-making has never flagged ! Not only that, but I was at the Rafinesque presentation with the Winhusen brothers at the Mohawk Gallery last evening -- I thought there was a chance you might be there, but then I learned you were still laid up. What say ye -- I could stop by any day... could even bring along an Eli's !

Ra 7/30/22 > I always suspected typos constituted a hidden touchstone where certain veins of contemporary poetry are concerned -- and you, sir, now stand revealed as being squarely in that grain . . . ! as for the noon hour, that's perfect since E's opens at 11 -- I could easily enough be knocking on your door, pulled porks in hand, at that hour. Again, it will be either Monday or Tuesday. By the way, do you realize how close you live to Jim Palmarini ? He's on the upper part of the Beechmont downslope not far from the new Tome Bookstore which is across B'mont from the Krogers.. I guess you're a mile or so past that?? two things : there will be a feature/open at the TOME Bookstore next Sunday at 6PM, Jim Palmarini's new hosting gig -- I could pick you up around 5:45 if you'd like... it's a good place; also, yeah, I do still want to read the revised & final version of the Addison review.

I lived in Manhattan from '62, right after high school, till '65, when I got drafted... Cassius Clay & Thelonius Monk were my touchstones back then (I did frequent the Village but no, Bob Dylan and the folkie revival was not on my radar) ... those two were the bellwethers, them and shooting pool in Times square, other areas, and on the Upper West Side... I'd heard tell of Charles Olson since the early '60s but didn't understand a word of him ... my awakening to the turbulent & multi-racial and anti-Nam protests/poetics of that era awaited my post-U.S. Army years on the G.I. Bill when at Kent State...

In that regard, the very last line of your Addison piece reverberated nicely with me, oh yes. as for Walter Benjamin, he pops up in your critical work frequently enough (you even mention him in regard to my own work!) that I'm ashamed to admit he is pretty much a black hole for me to this day -- my bad, no doubt.
Ty > Benjamin understood that insofar as art had replaced religion, in a post-religious Western world it had been endowed with quasi religious spirituality... hence the aura...

Ra > in your piece, you also used the word "aural" ... that stunned me, for it gave me a wholly differing take on the aura, yes? I have tried reading Addison's poetry aloud, but his radical re-tinkering with regard to individual line readings & word sequences makes for a somewhat clumsified stanzaic prosody -- the aural loses its aura in the lacerant & interruptus'd flow of sublime syllabic roughage, which I assume is utterly deliberate... it is language itself in his poetry that is the source of the umbra's disorienting effects on the poem -- so many of the individual lines wrest with grammatic vehemence, ouroboric in its effects to the point aurality is both devitiated & rendered aura-defunct (to my ear, at least) ... also, that somewhat rushed tangent using the "my sun" beginning seemed a fertile twist, particularly in its invoking of the Art Blakey recording -- I didn't want to see that line of inquiry/speculation moved away from quite so quickly, since it too seemed to have something provocative to offer with regard to the aural/aura vortex . . . hmmm - or should I phrase it "vortext" ?

Ty >   Thanks for these thoughts. I think you're right that Addison's grammatical and linguistic torques are designed to undermine the aural but I'd say an attack on one understanding of the aural, the usual metered reading per prosody....in brief, he is hearing the radical rhythms and sounds of bebop as rendered in, as, verse...

Ra's > looks to me like the usual metered reading's no more than a shade in his rear view, at least as far as the 7 pages of the umbra poem go, and as for Art Blakey, well, he's sent Addison permittedly off even bebop's thunder...

162

El Add's on his own, and what he hears only attendance at one of those Friday nights could prove . . . Sun/son, indeed.

so I take it the feature/open reading at the TOME Bookstore across the street from Krogers is not what interests you this Sunday ?

Ty and I could disagree : here following an apart-from Facebook joust, with Ty's review of my book litanies said handedly being our departure grimoire (of sorts) . . .

"Here, La Charity faces some of the same difficulties that we will see in Tracie Morris' most recent book, handholding, from Kore Press, which I will write about in my next post. It's a problem faced by all artists whose work is, ideally, inseparable from live performances: how to capture the "essence" of a live performance via recording or, more problematic, via translation into texts. Unlike Morris' book which directs the reader to a website of her reading from handholding, litanies said handedly includes no such redirection."

>>Big-time oversight, this one, since on page 129 there is a listing of two separate links to performance videos (those links can also be accessed via smartphone, if you have the relevant app, which is the meaning of those two strange glyph-squares to the right of each pic on that page).

"Litanies said handedly, a phrase that emphasizes

the relationship between vocality and manual manipulation, between articulation and inscription, is divided into three sections, each prefaced with one of La Charity's collages."

>>Well, the three sections are actually prefaced by four collages each, for a total in the book of an even dozen collages... given that the book contains 60 poems (NOT counting the poetry/prose construct that the back cover details), I should feel that the inclusion of those twelve collages constitute a significant element of the 'handedly' portion of the book's title. Also, "said handedly" somewhat pointedly refers to the visual dance of gestural amplification that pretty much always is there when I stand & deliver my memor-actualized raps at open readings . . .

Tyrone, the above are the two glaring errors, as excerpted from my original response to the review — if that response is no longer available to you, I can re-send it to you in its entirety. Just sent Robert the following : "Have contacted Tyrone about this, and he is willing to address the matter of making corrections regarding the two "glaring errors" ... not sure how that will play out with regard to the whole review appearing on the DM website, but he is willing -- I think, given his willingness to engage the matter, the two of you should talk . . . "

Why don't you two hash this out between you . . . it seems you two can, at this point, now forgo my bridge-building on this matter, yes ?

Ras adds more on the book : Yes, that back cover addendum is a significant one, for it amounts to a heads-up indicating a line of inquiry and provocation that might be taken up in the pursuit of why those collages are in the book at all. I have two thoughts about that : the collages are a graphic demonstration of the poet's compositional method as being physically grounded – they exemplify this poet's creative multi-dimensional breadth, how not only are the poems representative of the insistence on vocal proof, but visual proof as well, a sprung form of synesthesia that casts the collages as a kind of graphic poetics, one could even say visual jazz; plus, the collages challenge the reader – the way the poems in performance frequently defy comprehension, those collages do NOT have direct reference to the thematic substance of any of the poems… it is up to the beholder to intuitively establish that particular resonance, ie there are Furtherings to the act of poetry that find expression via the vividness of the setting… one could say that the collages are stand-ins for the audience factor, that the collages are witnessing agents, equally staring out at the beholder even as they graphically illuminate creative process. It can get pretty thick the further you take it, but that is precisely their function – they up the ante on the poetry experience of the book as a whole.

Some other of Ty's reactions you might find of nterest

La Charity's interest in, and performances with, jazz bands only reinforces his status as a direct descendant of the Beats. But unlike many of the Beats who read and performed in both non-academic and academic settings, La Charity has consistently refused to perform at colleges and universities. Litanies said handedly is thus a compilation of his poems and collages directed at non-academic audiences even if, truth be told, academics are more likely to read and enjoy this book than the bar, coffeehouse, and club patrons La Charity is known to favor.

>> This one could probably have taken a better direction if you and I had had more detailed conversations about my experience with jazz – are you referring to Kenneth Rexroth and Kenneth Patchen when you mention my performance ancestors, or maybe Bob Kaufman and Jack Micheline ?? Fact is, my experience with poetry & jazz was not one of coterie, genre, or influence … when I hit New York as a teen-ager in the early '60s, jazz was expressivity amplified quite beyond my previous experience and it amounted to a critical mass, specific gravity sort of nitty-gritty life-of-the-city phenomenon, inescapably so… I gravitated into the clubs as a riveted listener to the Thelonious Monk, Charles Mingus, Bill Evans, Miles Davis, John Coltrane, Rahsaan Roland Kirk kind of emerging music ferment & dynamism. What poetry I knew about at that time was exceedingly personal, and wholly rudimentary, not at all on my map as a public 'thing.' I was in the City for three years, never made the acquaintance of any poets, never saw a poet onstage as either a solo or as a sitting-in adjunct to the music – didn't happen. The music was a primary imprint, one that I more or less carried with me from Akron, where I first became aware of jazz as something worthy of

rapt attention – New York jazz was not only the big leagues, it was a life-giving revelation. And yeah, it was everything hip hop etc would be for a guy like, say, Napolean Maddox in the '90s. Your mention of Tupac is a valid contrast. Much as I came eventually to revere Beat poetry, to conflate my own work as being related to theirs is mostly a matter of critical convenience borne of apparency, rather than demonstrable linkage – I was, and remain, some other childe of the music I heard. In the '80s I was a member of a West Coast & Hawaii jazz ensemble as their poet, and in the '90s in Cinci was also a member of a jazz krewe, with Ken Leslie & Jack Walker in The Last Boppers, as a poet (Art Ensemble of Chicago influenced), and in the late '90s had my own jazz group, Sasemble, with Jack Walker and Dickie Williams mostly but we flexed to include others on occasion, ie James Quilligan, Anne Marie La Charity, Scott Hisey, Steve Lansky, and Bill Polak (with myself as the arranger, principal voice, and lead percussionist) – I performed both music as well as poetry with those groups, not exactly the imprint the Beats embodied. As for my consistent refusal to perform in academic settings, that one has mostly to do with the fact that, as you well know, readings in such settings are typically & woefully, non-dynamic – that, plus the fact that I left my only prolonged exposure to university yokage following the National Guard's appearance on the campus of Kent State University in the Spring of 1970 – Linda and I were present the day the students were shot down and I just never quite forgave & forgot. Universities, to this day, give me the willies, deeply so.

"To that extent then, La Charity reminds us that we who are fortunate to have hearing, first experience the world as pure sound before the necessity/desire for social contact and communication drives us to language acquisition."

>>This was notably expressed by you, brief but striking – do you have particular experience with anyone who suffered the loss or was born without the sense of hearing ??

"But as one may have already surmised, La Charity's project—which depends upon a defense of, and recitation from, memory as the connecting tissue or "umbilical" cord between utterance and self—is an aesthetic analogue to Walter Benjamin's various meditations on language and, in particular, translation. Just as La Charity insists that "Poetry" does not itself exist, that all poems are necessarily failed attempts to attain Poetry, so too for Benjamin all human languages aspire to the condition of Language. This religiosity will remind many of the modernists and those that follow in their wake, and thus it is not surprising that La Charity praises the efforts of Pound and Duncan, Williams and Spicer, all of whom, to varying extents, understood "poetry" as an exterior plane or realm (be it a premodern past, a spiritualized "parallel" reality, a local polis, or otherworldly dictation) from which the poets inhaled as inspiration and toward which their poems exhaled as utterance, breath, speech, etc."

>>You're really getting down to it with this shit – high concept interpretation, and I salute you for the Benjamin echo, which caught me by surprise. Gracias.

"But La Charity carefully distinguishes his oral/sound praxis from that of performance poetry, which he sees as unwittingly resurrecting the poet as priest via ego ... for La Charity, the poet reciting poems from memory is more like a conductor of a train, making sure that the whole thing doesn't come off the rails while making haste with due speed (La Charity emphasizes again and again the importance of rapid-fire delivery). And, of course, per his take down of storytelling and narrative on the first page of the manifesto, this train has no destination except Poetry—a final stop at which no poem arrives."

>>Good one. That whole matter of standing & delivering NOT as performance is for sure where I am located. At root, my own practice insists on both not-knowing AND searching-for. At my best, I'm a post-bop straight-ahead New York jazz-derived translator of expanded American idioms taken to rhapsodic extremes (Ray Bremser comes to mind as a brother poet in this regard... see his entry in the Allen anthology, The New American Poetry) and knowing where that train will end up just ain't part of the equation, or at least that was the way of it in my prime, whenever THAT was ! And in this regard the jazz exemplar extraordinaire who I would take as the signal practitioner most fertile for me would be John Coltrane . . . hours of daily lone working-thru is the Coltrane exemplum I adhere to.

"La Charity's apotheosis of sound as play follows the lead of that opening gambit in the first section, Splash Research, by opposing the implicit threat of idolatry associated with the fixed visual/landlocked (some poem titles are set in all caps) to the fluidity of water and sound."

>>Another good one. Neat that you picked up on the water/sound thing – and I would add that half the poems in that section, the ones that are titled in all-caps (tho' NOT that first poem, the VISIONAL one, which is meant to act as bridge between the visual, ie the collages, and the textual) are each meant to be recited in a single breath, from beginning to end… ideally, those twelve poems would take all of twelve deep breaths to recite. No way anybody'd know that if I didn't hip them to it, but that's the fact of it (I'm getting too long in tooth to actually recite them that way now, the lungs are simply too debauched at my age). Also, each of the twelve is a straight-on improv, based on a dialectic comprising two competing poles, the 'drums-a-woman' vs 'what're sharks' … ars poetica indeed, but with an improv demonstrum withal. As a final insight, that hour and a half solo ambuscade of a memor-actualized reading you attended at the Bonbonerie Cafe here in Cinci that sweltering August evening a few years back – it really was all of the 60 poems in the "said handedly" book, complete and in the exact same order that I followed, wholly from memory that evening in that presentation -- you are thus uniquely advantaged in having HEARD the WHOLE of the book, and in one long uninterrupted stream, eh ?

And finally, a few clips of note : https://www.facebook.com/ralph.lacharity/about_details

Extracted chat-bits
from Facebook give & take
betwixt Denis Mair and yours truly :

(from **Denis**, of the Pacific Northwest, starting 29 Nov '23:

INVITATION
(for Ralph La Charity)
the thousand-petalled bract invites you to its spin cycle...
the stream bed's tug hints at giddier declivities to come...
the rose may be distantly related to the flytrap...
pointers to the vortex appear by the wayside...
to loosen your tongue...put a trip in your step...
en route to the rounding of ends with beginnings...
no turning away from the festivity...
its electric branch-tips have sprung up inside you...
on a mission to gather what you will gather.
(Inspired by Ralph La Charity's "Happy Snappy at the
Brass Rail."
// The Brass Rail is a dive bar in Cincinnati.)

(**La Charity** responds :

for the good times . . .

so will he be good for something or good for
nothing was what they wondered them who
'd take us in I already knew this wouldn't end
well the bite shifts knees buckle & the grins
drift eyesight spotifies instability renders ver
dicts vastly disadvantageous you were ne'er
promised holiday turkey smooth sailing wake

up play piano take out the trash remember All
of all words is the biggest word the umbrella one
tricks nor felicitous curbs & roadbeds found e'er
newly autumnalized rogue scofflaw satellites in
exorably Voidward sans non-literate kooks' po
lity clan solitudinous lone shedster-shade calls
me Mishmated, old white wailer, me as bated

(from **Denis**, 19 Jan '24 :

UNTITLED
(in response to Ralph la Charity's poem about the word
scene in my home state Ohio, titled "not an artifice")

a particular kind of modernist exploratory engagement,
engaged in by those who proved themselves worthy
of having been born vocally equipped...
certainly the population flung across that stretch of land
had been explosively leavened by historical accelerants
and really needed to be made sense of,
not by fashionable theories,
but by being expressed in heart-searching speech...
I can imagine there was need for live vocal access
to the heart of that moment's experience,
by people whose ability to elicit each other's
heightened speech
proved that they belonged together.
I tasted only a bit of that later, out of state,
too late to live it as a full life arc.

(from **Denis**, 20 Jan '24 :

MY PART IN THE CONVERSATION
(inspired by Ralph La Charity's poem "respond/reply-")

What I need to heed this morning is a rousing call that
would snap me out of my "irritable reaching" and into
the light of day. I keep groping, by a chain of inferences,
for something "out there," trying to turn towards the
strength of a source-realm that undergirds me.

To me, the path of entelechy must record the wisdom
of a great composite being, which gathered ITSELF
together as IT started the functions of matter rolling,
and since then we've been along for the ride, part of
the slouching towards birth of creatures like ourselves
that can only bud off from IT.

But my search for faith in such matters is just my part
in a generation-spanning exchange, to which I am
forced to reply, because the issue of a transcendent
concern was injected into me by my history and
language. As a poet-friend wrote: "Even before it
was born, the eagle's gaze was nailed to the dome
of sky." But my part in the conversation about
that foundational entity (alias "Cosmic Man" or the
"Macranthrope") in no way mitigates my rightful
project of hollowing out a space, in a wintry season,
for singing, to the beat of my own heart, about the
here and now life-ordeal of self and confreres.

(**RLC** responds, same day :

>Denis included a reprinting of my poem, but as a run-on paragraph version with inner-text slash marks demarking the piece's original linebreaks.. after I reacted to his slashy reprint (alluded to below), he went back into his message and deleted his paragraphed copy, replacing it with a direct version of the poem as originally composed<

good that you reprinted the poem, Denis, but as for entelechy, I would take exception to reprinting the text as a paragraph with slashes -- the poem was composed as a 14-liner, each made line immediately stacked upon its preceding line to create an overall visual, that visual perhaps appearing much like a tombstone, or a pool table, or a backyard garden plot, depending on the field expedient vantage point of one's own reader's perspective... the 14 lines are all roughly the same length, which necessitates the occasional line break that occurs mid-word, which is occasionally briefly disorienting but ultimately deliberate & proscriptive. To reprint the poem as you have done reconstitutes the visual whole in ways that disguise & essentially deny the piece's architextual in-factitude, ie its meant integrity -- & that bothers me, so do click over to my own F'bk site to see the work as originally created . . .

(from **Denis**, 23 Jan '24 :

>here is the RLC poem to which Denis responded, comments below ...

because you asked –

springboard infusionings occurred discretely
how was I to know whiffs & whence without
time to delve thence whip-sluicedly unaligned
every Mind's its own Grand-pa these mycelial
terrors tramplified w/faux explicatudes held
abeyanced grainy/grey grinpot decadence de
adbeat reports hollow-sounded down empty
hallways in those toppled/recalled old hotels
long since vacant lottery'd down South Main
in shame-craven banks deprived of funda
mentasticized replicantankoried reflex
restitution resurrective illuminatival
gauntlets gainsaid upon slowly yoked
fade-outs grooved & no less certified..

>**RLC**'s addendum to that poem<

The Art of the Sprung is both public and oral. The
challenge when it comes to standing & delivering a
sprung 14-liner, which the above is, is to say the sprung
in its entirety by using a single deep breath -- failing that,
find out how many such breaths you need, then work at
reducing their number over time ... most sprungs take at
least three deep breaths, but many take more... the work
goes on.

>**Denis** goes where the following goes :

DENIZEN OF A DEEP DIVE
(in response to Ralph La Charity's poem "because you
asked," posted Jan. 22,)

Hipsterdom resorts to a seamy backdrop where the
shadows are studiedly blase towards all attempts to
chastise wastefulness, thus allowing cracks to form
in a moribund shell, opening a fourth space beneath
community, where the terminal cats gravitate
precisely because they receive no inducements. They
bring encouragement of their own--- be it a bottle or a
scene-making knack, or a pretzel of desire, performable
and unceasingly mutable.

The survivor nimbly rides the noospheric exhalations as
long as they last, in and out of venues,
gathering and contributing to the transpersonal nerve-
net ripples, shimmered over by the melodic cursor
of a waking dream, but having to wind down many
times, having to brave the chill of the rapport fading
time after time, to study for the next time, even while
walking away, to keep soaking in it and soaking it in,
taking on the freight which at the right moment is no
weight, holding a whole generation in little more than
a notion riding the air on a few filaments.

(from **Denis**, 25 January '24 :

>added still later, Denis reacts somewhat at length
to the poem beginning, "a lay's a language organism,"
which poem ends, "without left-lept en-Circe'd &/or
colloidal'd" <

A POEM AS LANGUAGE ORGANISM (1&2)
(in response to an untitled poem by Ralph La Charity)

176

1.
ROCKET ME OUT OF THIS PIT! ... That used to be my
internal cry. The alternative to improvisation would
have been boredom, and thank heavens boredom has
been repurposed as a launching pad... because the
cornered beast allowed its carcass to be parked too
long before death... and during its durance, its clotted
upwellings were ministered to by a miraculous spinning
wheel... thus laying out an inventory of sidewinding
ripple moves, ripe for combining... elicited by emptiness
that pregnantly promised that something would
hang on their thread... until the thing went forth
propulsively, endowed with the pride of its impetus...
ready to surprise its maker and to entertain in any
songfest it fits into.

2.
Your discourse... Your poem... needs replying to
more than once, because this reply did not touch on
the "extremities of refusal and affirmation peculiar
to distinct resonances." Also, the whole problem of
being colloidal is a double-edged pudding, because a
colloid within a living cell is poised at a tipping point
of liquefaction and solidification, where the phase
change allows for coordinated shifts of proximity,
linking embedded reactants in a ballet of unfolding
configurations. A poem as vehicle is vibratory yet
reticent, because it represents the fusion of a particular
"radiative interlock"... Even so it lets you know where
it stands, confronting you with "extremities of refusal
and affirmation peculiar to distinct resonances," and
proud of its identity, having been fully open to "ripples

of Else" throughout its gestation, all of which fed into its ingrown maturation as a uniquely choreographed specimen of "local elan," refusing reductionism, but tempting one to bounce something against it, and lending itself to paraphrase, as I am doing in this reply. As for the (dis-)advantages of being congealed or not, and as for the issue of being seized or not by Circe's ensorcellments, the whole question of being colloidal is a double-edged pudding, because a colloid within a living cell stays near the tipping point... Its layers are poised between liquefaction and solidification, letting embedded reactants slide toward or away from each other in balletic formations, and as for the dangers of enthrallment by Circe, it depends on whether the truffles being rooted for are hidden in celestial or terrestrial soil./ DCM

RLC responds : You say it very well, Denis . . . nuff said !

(from **Denis**, 7 Feb '24 :

CRUISIN WITH WORD JAZZ
   ---for Ralph La Charity
    ("it's harrowing to have to rediscover
      a poem's Being & to have to re-dedicate
      oneself to delivering its Essence aloud..." Ralph La Charity)

Ah to be the field o'er which tines are scoured, and dust raised and brow mopped...
ah to tunnel out from recalcitrance and sequentialize

the stations of a sleighride...
I'm talking about the kind of sleighride when wolves
were nipping right behind
And when Antonia heard that story, she pressed her
skinny body against you
I'm talking about a sleighride of the neural Nantucket
kind,
experienced by an English major reading MOBY DICK
for the third time
Ah to find the right proprioceptive sketch that keys
into the gnarl
ah for a Komodo dragon's practiced run that deftly
outruns its prey
ah to be party to the commotion and rambunction
of a melody-jointed contraption
louring down upon its glidepath....
ah to re-desynchronize the sonic terrain and traverse it
in headlong hurtle...
ah the elusive bells of celestial pathways in the
interstices of earthly sound...
oh the instantaneous chimerical joining of falling and
calling...
until the last flourish of retro-rockets sets the pod
down lightly
upon a re-envisioned surface,
kited and spooled back,
off-world and on-site.

(**RLC**'s respo, same day :

so much to weigh, in how you've worded this, Denis..
to be cast between the Devil & the deep blue sea was

more or less my initial take -- between derivations &
the original See was the next take.. and it has gone on
that way, changing oddly, but changing inexorably,
each time that I re-approach all that your wording
does.. it's unstable & steady state simultane, the Whale/
Wail Splashdown, supple nonetheless.

Another recent message from **Denis**, 2nd week o Feb 2024 :

It's been great sharing during this streak, a streak such
as I have never had. A few artists vivified my eyes
(namely Nico Vassilakis, Aram Chaled Res, Abdelhaq
Djellab and Sanju Paul). They actually infused creativity
straight in through my eyeballs to kick start the streak..
And the quiddity of your language/engagements did
it for me too, so you were very much part of the mix.
And Bree has added an irreplaceable note too, made me
aspire to have a bit of that Kentucky lilt rub off on me.
So I had forty or so poems I'm proud of in a 3-4 month
period around my 72nd birthday. Now I have to pull
my straw hatbrim a bit lower over my eyes and do a
couple of sizable editing projects for livelihood, so I'm
going to step back awhile, maybe wind down a bit, but
I've convinced myself of what's possible. I'm convinced
it can come again. During this streak there have been
some pretty positive influences so it's a good vibe for
me as I turn to some grunt work.

La Charity's response > ... yea, Denis -- go back to your
"other" work now, assured that we've just had quite the
fertile run... many thanks, mi companero !

A new prompt from **Denis**, prior to the 2024 edition of
the Kent Open Poetry Festival (Jawbone) :

It would be nice to read an account of what happened
after you met with your wife Linda's freshman English
teacher Maj Ragain at a bar in Kent. From fragmentary
readings on your timeline, I understand that you were
pretty much in on the ground floor of the Kent poetry
festival and scene.

RLC responds, 4/15/2024 > When Major and I first
met we were both still in our 20s, May 4th 1970 hadn't
happened yet, and we had yet to write the kinds of
poetry we would have to write if we wanted to keep
at it after we entered our 30s ... as for ground floors,
yeah -- when Linda & I finally left Kent in '76, we said
farewell to an array of possibilities those friends &
collaborators we'd known & had engaged with, some
of whom went on to put down roots thereabouts, who
would variously harvest for decades thereafter... your
year on the main campus was actually the same 1973
when Shelly's Book Bar, at the corner of Summit &
Franklin in town, became the center of the burgeoning
Kent Area Poets off-campus combine, publishing its
first magazine, with several ensuing editions to come,
initiating an independent effort that was to last for
decades & result in dozens of off-campus events &
poets' book publishings. Some of this is referred to in
my 2019 Dos Madres book, BLOOD VERTIGO, which
also contains my farewellia a la old friend Major.
The current steward for off-campus poet shenanigans

would be poet/naturalist RC Wilson : https://www.
facebook.com/poettree1953 ... RC's contributions date
back to my own public beginnings there in Kent -- we
also knew each other for several years when he lived in
Berkeley CA, when his wife Camille was pursuing grad
school out thereabouts. RC's tenure as the latest Kent
Area poet & scene ringleader is notable for his embrace
back to the University, whilst still keeping active as an
independent "townie." Major also embraced the back
to the big school on the Hill -- I never did.
Kent's off-campus independent Open Poetry Festival's
been occurring in Kent for better than thirty years
running – it always occurs on the three-day weekend
closest to May 4th, annually... after its being begun by
poet Bill Polak over the course of three years, 1988-90,
we called the Fest the April Aegis / ALOUD ALLOWED.
Major took responsibility for keeping that Open Poetry
Festival alive, over the years from 1992 till his death in
2017 – he renamed the Fest the JAWBONE.
https://www.facebook.com/photo?fbid=262118791470
9696&set=a.730645607097279

Denis responds > Thanks for the useful info.
My high school buddy Dean Kahler was shot and
paralyzed on May 4. Later he went on to be a
wheelchair BB player and commissioner of Athens
County :
https://www.poemhunter.com/poem/may-fourth-in-
memoriam/ . . . (reprint follows below :

May Fourth, In Memoriam

May Fourth happened twenty miles from me,

That's what brought the war home.
My high school friend got shot in the back,
That's when it hit me that there was a war.

Dean Kahler was a Mennonite who grew up on a farm;
We understood each other; we were the only two
Who reminded everyone in our civics class
That the Vietnamese didn't want us on their soil.
He served two years as a conscientious objector,
Worked in a hospital, got himself a Japanese girlfriend.

Then Dean went to Kent State, took classes at the main campus.
There was a pulse beating there, at the forefront of the times,
The James Gang played at bars on Water Street,
The young professors were radical and involved.
I went to a branch campus, an overgrown high school;
I didn't know what Main Campus had been up to
To get itself occupied by the National Guard;
Local papers didn't do much to clue us in;
The authorities were keeping the war contained.
I'm afraid I was off in my own world,
I went off camping while classes were canceled,
Smoking marijuana alone in the woods,
Getting swallowed up in green solitude.
But then I thumbed a ride home from the State Forest
And the state employee who picked me up said,
"They killed some demonstrators in Kent, it's about time, "
And I kept quiet until we got to Canton.
Later I saw the pictures, Guardsman dressed in combat gear,

As if they had gone in to clear out a jungle village,
They charged around campus in snouted masks,
The war had finally escaped from its jar.
Dean Kahler was shot, 320 feet from the Guardsmen,
As he watched from the edge of the Commons,
He had turned to run at the sound of gunfire.
The Guardsmen had a line of fire downhill
When they killed Allison at the base of the knoll.
No stray bullet severed Dean Kahler's spine.
It had to be a trajectory of hate, peppering the crowd
To let all the demonstrators know
What bad-assed killing machines they were.
That was when everything became serious,
That shocked me into to wanting to know the reasons:
Ohio was not just a place of rolling corn fields;
The corn of Ohio had raised two kinds of people,
And one kind hated the other.
That day the hidden death-trigger showed itself,
Who knew what could set it off again?

Dean Kahler went through some low times,
Hooked up to tubes in his bed,
But he was made of something strong,
His face was not made to glower with hatred.
With the settlement money he bought himself a car
With a gas pedal on the steering column.
He visited the families of the dead;
He formed a network of survivors;
He gathered archives about the shooting
For the university where he was shot.
He kept demonstrating against the war.
He gave up his plan to go to Japan.

He drove around the state, an activist for the handicapped.
He found a new girlfriend, he finished his degree.
He played wheelchair basketball,
He collected music, played tapes of Leonard Cohen;
How he could keep from being swamped by negativity,
Sitting in that wheelchair hearing music
That went straight to the chasm of the soul?
But he charged ahead and collected friends,
He settled down in Athens County:
That was Ohio's own little corner of Appalachian anarchy.
He was always at a downtown tavern on Friday afternoons,
Presiding at beery social gatherings near the Courthouse.
He knew the professors at the college
And dope growers who lived in the hills.
The locals embraced him as one of their own
And ended up electing him County Commissioner.
I went for a visit, and he took me to his haunts
I came away thinking, maybe his body had been shattered,
But his spirit was more whole than mine.

-Denis Mair.

La Charity signs off > "They charged around campus
in snouted masks" ... they did indeed, but I always recall
that not all the Guardsmen fired directly at the slain
students -- even in their ranks, the division between
what hate did, and/or didn't do, prevailed ... me and
Linda were there, on campus witnesses that day along
with a few thousand others ... we are the both of us
Nam-era US Army vets, but my own on again off again
allegiance to the Powers that be never managed to stir

anew afterwards, it all ended on that defining day, for the both of us. I've been able to cycle back to Kent many times over the many years since 4 May 1970, but my public commitment to independent Kent Area Poetries had its inception precisely there & then . . .

Resumes- from **RLC**, July 12, '24 :

Friday morning sundown :
In my imagination I can create another world... but I cannot sustain myself in that other world. Nor am I able in that imagined other world to grow actual food that will feed anybody, not even insects. But of course, in my imagination, I can even grow imaginary food, food even insects can eat, and we all know insects can eat just about any kind of food, maybe even imaginary food. Most particularly if they are imaginary insects, eh ? We all know imaginary insects can eat anything and everything, food or not. And unless I am mistaken, created other worlds of the imagination teem with hungry bugs just like that.

Response from **Denis** :

THINGS IN IMAGINATION
  (pinging back at Ralph La Charity's prose poem titled "Friday Morning Sundown")

Things in imagination can go in any direction. The fourth wall of an imaginary enclosure can be a picture window of transparent icing, but there is nothing there to eat the scene, except presumably the space itself. The space- evoking medium prefers axes that extend by antic wishfulness, hence the sugar icing windows are consumed by fleeting appreciation, and there is no imaginary metabolism to be cloyed by consequences. The cloud sculptures are extended by breezy puffs of expectancy, and they scatter as easily as they form. Wasps suddenly house themselves in wasp-cud, with no need to rehearse the procurement of woody mouthfuls and other papermaking procedures. The proper functioning of feelings in imagination is intended to be leonine. The wasps can immerse themselves in solicitude for the brood, which is their dreamed-of role, so they are spared the need for sub-imaginings of black mold that undermines papier-mache. Unless of course the imagination is hag-ridden, but that veers to nightmare. Normally it is whimsically extensible and readily switches scenes, so that the notional stream exhibits healthy flexibility. There is, however, a predictable quotidian tragedy, namely the frequent mis-assignment of a rapporteur who is overly bureaucratic, whereupon too many of the delicious plot-twists and icing details are lost. A healthy functioning brain, having been burned by the bureaucrat one too many times, will be wily enough to assign an antic editor who can spin those boilerplate reports in a clownish way, and that too is part of the overall imaginary enterprise.

La Charity responds : the bureaucratic rapporteur quickens into existence the faux poet, both of whom conspire to coalesce into a Further Foundation, one that both weans & proscribes... strategic aesthetic intelligence requires us not only to fiddle while Rome burns, but also to beware the groaning board of expanded awarenesses -- you can't get here from there, yet it simultaneously seems you can . . .

MORE-THAN-RECKLESS EYEBALLING
as of late October 2024
(Inspired by Ralph La Charity's poem titled "Victory"**)

The drama has been ratcheted up to a huge scale.
Seen from our individual eyes, how can collective forces be anything but blind?
Yet they slouch their way toward parity and deadlock,
as if by adversarial physiology of a two headed leviathan,
and we are Jonahs looking out (and looking out for ourselves, we hope).
What delirium is like the sense of that deadlock breaking?
We have known such dreadful distraction and it has shaped our days.
How can the cubist fur and bone-crunching pivots of such a shaggy beast
be gathered fully into affronted retinas?
By the more-than-reckless eyeballing of beauty's love turned meta...
(and beyond that kiting from meta to meta),
than which there is no more honest poetics,
to which the poem that prompted this note attests.

Correspondence update as of mid-January, 2025 :

from **Denis** :

A SALUTARY VEIN OF MYSTICAL THINKING
(growing out of exchanges with Ralph La Charity on FB)

We have to beware that mystery doesn't get appropriated as a beast by the ravening Beast. We are laboring under large insufficiencies and are failing to deliver the right information on a large conveyor belt, namely nutriment that young minds can gnaw on to rework themselves while avoiding pitfalls into the obscure and insufficiently worried hide of Leviathan. Relationship pulp can be left to Harlequin, and the court of love deserves an Eleanor worthy of respect, but in any case there are cautionary cases of emotional snarls, and their stories should be sounded like foghorns. Reason needs clear sightings and soundings as befits a helmsman's role. Any traffic I have with mystery should, I hope, be chalked up on the side of existence as the basic grubstake for any excavation. By mining it we learn to put an inner vista into our formulations, to imbue them with space for resonance that still thrums with originative life force.* In other words, any spelling done with the unincluded should be a ratchet of receptivity towards the unknown as underpinning and source of all endowments, hence auguring towards awe or even gratitude. In other words working with what one has and being glad to get the chance. (I hope.) In other words, amor fati towards the fati that could have been, even though this one is turning incredibly perverse, jumbled and grinding like rocks ready to shift. As for the existential side of the ledger, we are the ones who got this grubstake to mine what we can. We are the local agents who decide whether to go it alone or throw in our lot with lesser or larger collectives, and from here on we are responsible. As in Sartre. I'm talking about walking on two legs (as Mao used to say). On one side is the mystery leg, so we can get a leg up by considering mere existence a net gain over nothing at all, a tournament in which we hold the first win that was already won before we knew we were players. Now it's up to us. If mysticism doesn't at least augur and/or militate in the direction of awed ("odd"?) enlivenment, then it isn't worth a rat's ass. And as a matter of fact, the givenness-as-gain aspect of mystery can be seen in in a ratty place as well as anywhere else. As for the other leg, it's Sartrean all the way, taking things upon oneself and not blaming others. It's a matter of making cagey choices, motivating each other and transferring huge conveyor belts of needed information to each other at critical times. And don't go holding demonstrations where people are going to shoot us mercilessly. In other words try to keep safe (in a mystery blind for viewing wildlife) and thrash things out for ourselves.

from **Ralph** : Where is the poetry ? As I've said elsewhere, ALL poets fail at poetry. What we of the ancient calling manage to do, ever & always, is attempts at poetry. To say poetry isn't there is, at best, a wholly other kind of failure, based on fast & facile dismissals themselves based solely on the compulsion to render a verdict. If the poem does not resonate as poetry for you, all that means is that failure itself once again has risen up, dancing in the interstices -- you are but failure's dancing partner. Verdicts you levy moulder obliquely, at best - one grum preordained failure overlain by another. No news there.

from **Denis** : It's a curious kind of rainbow that appears
only when you're chasing it, but when you stop to look
it won't peep out for you. To resound in other minds,
you yourself have to be the collective mind thinking,
but you are after all only yourself. Mere ratiocination
is a shell. All your emotivity can do is push around the
game tokens of your individual mind, hoping that they
chime with the emotivity of the collective mind. When
the game tokens of the collective mind move, everyone
is the audience.

from **Ralph** :   mebbe, but then again . . .

I have come to tell you all I cannot tell
y'all all at all – all a-yawn, I yaw
the yawp the yawl's oars allude, such
stuff & stutter, how the ear grabs in such
seizures of quasi-whimsy, such indutiful
truancy, its very lure elastic & tangy yet
of an elusivity, too, tho' usually unpursued

great awl, word-tap's omen-owl law-cowled;
glut of reason, so much left out, utterly;
strop-wit alacrity & acuity, wholly uncured;
let us now resist the leaving out of things,
let's work the abundant hide of secrecy, how
the here & now herds the ear's flummoxen,
how secrecy stamps its hooves relentlessly
& how mystery's clove wags reason's
prejudicial inefficiency like a bent cue

.. yea, being alone is both unavoidable & omnipresent
-- ever in the midst of an enveloping swarm, to choose

is still the singular option mobilesse oblige bequeaths . . .
mobilesse oblige will overcome !

from **Denis** : "mobilesse oblige" is absolutely a cool
concept. I imagine it being coined during session of
repartee at the Brass Rail, or perhaps while preparing
to bust a move outta Dodge with your better half.
My father would have liked such a concept. On more
than on occasion he remarked that "noblesse oblige"
was his fate due to the "droit de seigneur" that was
asserted upon one of his recent female ancestors by a
bearer of the local nobility's bloodline. Being singled
out to receive a drop of blue blood, the powers above
expected him to put his abilities to use providing for
a family and relatives. He had to keep on plowing his
father's field even after he got married. A picture of
my Dad's home village lent credibility to his surmises.
A picturesque ruin of a castle overlooked the village,
perhaps the seat of the very bloodline of which he
spoke.

from **Ralph** : while in then-West Germany for 3 years
in the '80s, we lived in Landstuhl, a small town close
to Ramstein Air Base that had the ruins of a castle on a
bluff above the ville - your last sentence above brought
it back to mind. Your mention of the Brass Rail put me
in mind of an adult dancer bar in Newport KY, across
the Ohio River from downtown Cincinnati, called the
Brass Ass - your 2nd sentence above brought the Ass
back to mind also. As for the term "mobilesse oblige,"
that term is my own, coined sometime during my years
of roaming as mobility-obligated open poetry operative
hither & yon in cities across Amerisha's abundant hide,

to include extended stays in Denver, San Antonio, San Franscisco, Seattle, & now Cinci -- even had a notable sojourn over in Honolulu, once upon a time. Your post took me down one very protracted & sonically well-articulated memory lane -- thank you !

Denis responds : This account of peregrinations sounds wonderfully free-wheeling. It also has sizable dimensions and articulations like a tree laid out horizontal across the land. It has grand branchings and exploratory probings like a tree gradually occupying a space in the upper canopy. But in your case, it claims not the lofty overstory but the land's amplitude. No wonder you come up with phrases like the land's "abundant hide" (whatever the adjective may be). And as you say it lends itself to sweeping sonic evocations, because the arcs of its course call for a canticled narrative. You've measured it with the length of your staff. And like a tree that gives a special expansive view of the horizontal, by offering its branches held aloft, your horizontal tower offers a privileged vantage point on the vertical. You can survey all metaphors of ascending levels of abstraction (i.e., metaphysics) and see what contortions people get into while trying to occupy them concretely.

Didn't you leave New York out of your list of cities lived in? And heaven forfend the omission of Akron !

Ralph concludes : Yes, some of my itinerary was omitted, but only because standing & delivering in public as a poet had yet to become my modus operandi -- from 1968, I attended Kent State University on the

G.I.Bill, and it was in the fall of 1970 (subsequent to the May 4th murders by the National Guard troops on the campus, which my wife Linda and I were both present for) that my public poetry practice emerged & became a signature factor from then on. Those cities listed above were urban activist locales for me years after my times in Akron and Manhattan.

Of a MOTR feature/open in Cinci one Sunday evening in late August 2024 :

So what do you do if you & a pal or two decide to
stop by your local tavern one Sunday evening for
some modest tippling & conversation, but when you
get there, the stage is occupied by poets on mic (it's
an open poetry reading!) and the sound system is
amplifying their speech so that it's every bit as loud
as your & your friends' converse ? You might not
even stay long enough to order a single round would
be my guess, since poetry, whether it's open poetry
or featured poets, just ain't what you came in for. Or
suppose you did come for the poetry, since you are
both a poet yourself and a supporter of open poetry
in general, but the featured poets that night brought
their own coterie of at least a hardcore dozen or so
supporters, many of whom also had verse to deliver on
mic, all of whom were greeted by enthusiastic support
from that same coterie, since it seemed they were all
pals of a kind from previous events of a similar nature
elsewhere… ? Given the coterie's mostly non-critical
enthusiasm for the verse assertions of their fellow
versifiers, you might be forgiven for assuming the
reading's assembly that night might have had a kind of
locked-in bias… given those apparent odds, you might
find yourself somewhat abashed, even intimidated,
by the prospect of finding acceptance for your own
poetry offerings, particularly if the coterie's poetics
bandwidth was at a certain variance from your own –
after all, what matters most at any open poetry reading

is the quality of the listening any audience is able to extend to strangers who have gumption enough to stand & deliver on mic. So it went at yesterday evening's monthly feature/open poetry gathering at Cinci's MOTR Pub. The real test was not that the coterie was so self-contained, no, rather it was that the poetry itself was not necessarily what the coterie was there for... they were there to support each other. Poetry might be their ostensible group identifier, but cheering for each other's efforts was the group's modal bottom line. Was the night a success or not, you might wonder, and all I can honestly reply is, well... "iffy" at best. You would have to consult with each individual listener, since listening was the even deeper bottom line, as it always is at poetry events, and true listening is always a matter of one auditor at a time, simultaneously. If you could listen for poetry, beyond the mere hearing of verse self-expression, you probably stayed to the end – you probably even heard some of what you came for. It was a steamy night in the City, it lasted about two hours, and it was still daylight but the gloaming was encroaching when we finally hit the bricks.

Pauletta Hansel (Cincinnati, OH) :
I hear you.

Bill Kennedy (Cleveland, OH) :
A reading back in the day at a small venue in Tremont. The sound system was not working and another poet came by and said "If it's good they will listen." Then promptly plugged his banjo into an amp to accompany his reading.....

Reply, **Ralph La Charity (Cincinnati, OH)** :
.. things can go awry, oh ain't it so . . .

Al Milburn (SF Bay Area, CA):
Amplify ampfully and fools rush in...to listen?

Reply, **Ralph** : MOTR is a remarkable venue for sound
and our usual sound man, Mark Flanigan, knows what
he's doing, but there are never any guarantees when
the mic is open : what goes in will come out & never
the twain, eh ? Not that there wasn't actual poetry
now & then last night, just that the lack of guarantees
got the upper hand early on somehow & it was much
tough sledding from then on . . .

Agram Bigsby (Cleveland, OH) :
More power to them, literally. More power to any
group that supports each other in creative endeavors.
An open stage is a training ground, not a museum.
The volume lets freak flags fly, which is what
creativity sometimes needs, if only as a "hell, yeah,"
because there's a hell without that yeah out there
hunting us all.

Reply, **Ralph** : and more power back atcha, AgB -- in
retrospect, maybe I should have been more thrilled,
but it was hard. For me, poetry is something I have yet
to hear, heard... it's something you recognize when it
shows up, volunteer & blindside. And it is just woefully
easy to drown such things out, since they are usually
ever so brief & even more easily missed, unless you're
listening closely... & poets, too, even as they read

Jefferson Carter (Tucson, AZ) :

Ralph, "If you could listen for poetry, beyond the mere hearing of verse self-expression"? Verse self-expression IS poetry. The term "poetry" does not mean something wonderful in itself. If that wuz true, there'd be no such thing as bad poetry. "Verse self-expression" may be BAD poetry, but it's still POETRY.

reply, **Ralph** : how fatuous of you, Jefferson, to skip so blithely by a distinction between poetry & verse with the notion that discerning the BAD wouldn't affect the fact that the blood coming from your ears was due to what was being heard rather than what claimed itself as being the art of poetry ... we hear the lack of poetry everywhere, but its arrival occurs only if we are listening is closer to the distinction I was trying to make (and evidently failing to make

reply **Jefferson** : Ralph, ouchie! "Fatuous" is one of my fav words! Anyway, I've been pushing for a definition of poetry forever but getting nowhere with all my poetic friends. Seems as if poetry is some magic, supernatural elixir that various containers contain. Almost all the popular definitions are definitions of GOOD poetry, not poetry in itself. Care to lay your definition on this desperate pedant? XO

reply **Ralph** : I've lost track of how many poetry chapbooks you've published, Jefferson, and word has it that you are employed as a teacher of poetry there in Tucson, so I've assumed you're asking for someone else's definition of poetry is a rhetorical ploy.

Either you are predisposed about such a definition, or you're just being cute when you ask, but either way, don't we both know that such a definition depends on who you are asking -- from neophytes to old hands, the answer will be both provisional & unstable... it's that perdurable distinction between hitting a stationary target or a moving target, as perpetrated by a stationary shooter or one mounted on moving horseback -- as for "poetry," what use would defining the term be if the conditional factors aren't both rigorously specific and loosely non-repetitive ? Sounds paradoxical. Like what is the sound of one mouth uttering two or more realities simultaneously, neither nor none of which exist necessarily within the other's(s') purview . . . & of course from there it only gets more complex, depending on the patience & tolerance of the given interlocutors. And yeah, I am being cute with my reply . . .

Bree Zlee Bodnar (Geauga County, OH) :
Are you saying that it felt more like a support group than a poetry reading?

reply **Ralph** : Bree, see Agram's comment, above ... and yes, that was the evening's principal drift.

reply **Bree** : I can see a lot of sides of that coin

reply **Ralph** : .. oh yes, the possibilities do just go on & on - I've probably never been to a reading that wasn't a social occasion, so yeah, support is a goes-without-saying necessity at such events, but where variety

comes in is where this particular social occasion gets to be so peculiarly beguiling. Support itself is in the soul of the receiver, something we actually give to ourselves - what an audience does is let furtherance beyond self-support become operative. All bets are "on" when we step up to deliver in public - whatever else may be working in such occasions, rest assured the voluntary participation of each poet has both the fear-of & the courting-of the Unknown as a contributing factor, and is maybe even the most significant factor, yes ?? At an open poetry reading, none of the possible effective factors is guaranteed, but all find their way into the mix : each poet is the First Poet ... each poet is the Last Poet. An audience gives its support and, in the best of all possible Unknown open poetry worlds, the Poet returns the favor by taking their breath away.
reply Bree : can't even reply you said it all so well
reply Jefferson Carter : .. Bree, many of the community readings I attend are exactly that -- gatherings of wounded sensitive plants sheltering in a SAFE SPACE!

Jim Palmarini (Cincinnati, OH) :
Having tried and tried over the years to stay steadfast with my ears and cognition on auditory of each poet in recitation, I have learned to tune out MOTR din moments during Word readings... until I can't. Given the now considerable history of the series in the venue's "main" room such challenges have been remarkably limited. In 2016, when the reading series was 2 years old and still confined to MOTR's basement Sword Room, only a quirk in the house's scheduling (a comedy event, I think) pushed us upstairs for the

night. We were expected to return to the cavern the next month as there was management hand wringing that the poets would disturb the customers. But I knew there was no going back. And we didn't. MOTR has remained a gracious host all these years. There will always be regulars and the curious in and out during a main street stroll. Some will listen to the poets, others not. I'm okay with that—it's a bar with open arms for all and I'm grateful for that.

reply **Ralph** : .. bars are bars, eh ? To be sure, any poet who shows up for a poetry open mic with the intention of participating in the flow of what's happening mustneeds tread carefully, with ears wide open for what might or might not be appropriate to offer -- last night I did see a number of poets who cancelled their own intent to participate, based apparently on what was being presented on that mic. A few of them stayed there, listening till the night ended. You stayed because as host you had to, I stayed because I figured there was always a chance I'd get to witness something my listening ears had never heard before. The paradox was resonant all the way thru . . .

Barry Be (Cuyahoga Falls, OH) :
Ralph La Charity and Jim Palmarini: Been there, too, of course, mostly in music, and what I can say is that if the people in the audience aren't aware enough to remove themselves in DISTANCE from the center of the moment's attention, well, they just don't care or "get it" and I find that to be very selfish, myself. Yes, we aren't perfect: I and I bet you have lost ourselves for a

few moments, but NOT a whole night, and let me tell you, when I run into it I intentionally start screaming what I'm doing because 90% of the time it wakes folks up to the ridiculousness of what they're doing in the audience and if not, yeah it IS then time to go, but not w/o a few well-chosen words for the host. Popularity be damned at such a point. Vapid is vapid, and we all need to ensure that REASON prevails, or why bother with it at all, eh?

Jefferson Carter :
.. Jim, as long as the not so curious SHUT THE FUCK UP!

Tony Green (Auckland, New Zealand) :
that's is similar to what happened in Auckland to open mic readings of poetry - & prose in the 2000s - readings founded by people who were dissidents from the standardized academic teaching - what you might call 'experimental' -- were overtaken by a popularist crowd who were hostile to both the academies mainstream poets who published books & the writers who were 'experimental' -- they were kind of anti-intellectual brown-shirt crowd encouraged by the right wing neo-liberal politicians who had taken control of the education system & the patronage of the arts in the 1990s. Some 'open' mic readings were set up by the only State patron remaining - or heavily influenced on the committee - by Creative NZ. In the 80s I cd read at the University at Folk clubs at Folk Festivals in art galleries no trouble -- Having been excluded from the Universities by the Government people in the 1990s I cdn't read anywhere else - except at the old radical

dissident "Poetry Live" that had moved from The Globe to The Thirsty Dog - I was surprised to find I was out of place from the start - reading from my poetry-tubes - & some of the controlling committee were fairly hostile - but I persisted for two months before I could get a hearing - & by then I had made a few friends on the committee. I read every week there for a year. I finally gave up when it became dangerous - I told the committee I wouldn't read there unless they could guarantee my safety from the thugs that had begun to turn up. You understand that the arts scene in Auckland is very much like what you'd see as provincial. Reply Ralph : ... such a report, Tony -- no brown shirts here at the MOTR series, but the old biker motto still applies : stay alert, stay alive . . .

Dennis Formento (Slidell, LA) :
that's the problem with the open mike. Now that everybody is truly a poet, all you need is Instagram, it is indeed tough tobogganing. Sharon Messmer posted a frightening dispatch on FB a couple days ago saying that even her own NYU students do not want to read "outside of their experience" if at all. What becomes of true "diversity" when you don't read outside of your own limited experience? And as for poetry== it becomes blank-faced prose or the same thudding rhythms unsubtle enough for the untrained ear. I'm not becoming an elitist, I'm becoming a bearcat for the unread.

reply **Ralph** : .. I expect you're learning to carry that wealth of experience so many years in the trenches has piled up within you, which is me, too ... life itself becomes our training ground, inevitably enough, and then we move off from it all, eh ?

La Charity's post-addendum to the above, per alles : A crucial & indispensable dispensation in the poet's office is Memory & the public Practice & Demonstra thereof, as dutiful extension of that office for as long as the poet is able. Yea, and "echoes" is the big word, same way "mirrors" is... and my own latest preferred term is "resonance," wherein it is an all-sides immersive & inclusive totality we get to swim thru constantly -- how could time/history be any different, eh ? Stay alert, stay alive, indeed, as was always how the bikers would put it . . . yes ?

Again - Where is the poetry ? As I've said elsewhere (in some other earlier book?) ALL poets fail at poetry. What we of the ancient calling manage to do, ever & always, is attempts at poetry. To say poetry isn't there is, at best, a wholly other kind of failure, based on fast & more often than not facile dismissals, themselves based solely on the compulsion to render a verdict. If the poem does not resonate as poetry for you, all that means is that failure itself once again has risen up, dancing in the interstices -- you are but failure's dancing partner. Verdicts you levy moulder obliquely, at best - one grum preordained failure overlain by another.

No news there.

Farewellia a la post-Sprungs :

hey, Klyd . . .

yes I got yr review request & book overview with the
PDF etc

and I found it a tad too confounding to negotiate the
poems in the format as formatted — kept skipping
about uncontrollably just when I'd be getting
interested in one or the other individual piece !
Not my cup of tea when it comes to reading such a
collection of your work - I'll just have to wait to read it
in book form I guess.

Whether or not I'd ever want to issue a review, well ...
probably not is about the most honest reply I can give.
Reviews are odd things — are they love notes ? Are
they pimp notes ?? Do they illuminate the poetry.. do
they lend ballast to the equation or do they just put
undue emphasis on the reviewer's own acumen ? Hell,
my dear man — maybe all they really do is encourage
the poets to persist, which I should think would
actually be their best result — someone out there gets
it, or at least gets an indicated significant part of it,
yeah... and "this here review is the genuine proof of
that" eh ? Everybody gets a boost. Mebbe.

I'm just about at the same point you are in that my own
next book has its dear publisher lined up, the contents
decided upon, sometime this year it will come out... yea,

& what then ? Another in that line of the unread, most of it to moulder in boxes in my closet, unheralded . . . we all face these terrible moments of near despair, waiting for the books to be completed as objects in hand, proof of our continuing labors in the field.

I've always given more of my books away than ever sold many... I can't see that changing, no matter who does or doesn't review it. Your request breaks my heart, Klyd, it just does.

Ah but, I do look forward to trading mine for yours when the time comes, you bet, somewhere on down the line. And I trust you are of similar mind . . .

-Ra's.

Klyd Watkins (Nashville, TN) responds :

hell yes   I give them away at the rate of 10 to 1 (here I go making up statistics again--it's higher than that) I did not realize that the PDF I sent wouldn't behave but I shd have.   The digital or physical ARCs I hope are better
But your response is perfect
No one has done a better job than you at realizing where poetry lives today is at the readings and positioning yourself and yr ever changing audience to receive its energy that way   You can use that as a blurb if you ever need to

La Charity concludes :

thanks for your generous reply, Klyd...

over the course of my time up to this, my 80th year,
I've yet to use blurbs on my books — at best, I'll run a
quote from inside the book's poems, but damn ! if ever
I were to run a good one, yours would be the one.

-Razul.

the latest last Open Poetry poem

for what is ear
if not Mental Spirit, o poet,
& what is tongue

    save Ejaculate Grave, opened ?

for it is sound as meant & moving spin
that moves upon the skin & moves the limbs
is sound skinny & plump & meant mobile as
ivory against the woods that roll &
mobile meant in airs fallen heir to
spun cloth rent & the reigns reined

here we spin upon the plain
our feathering rapt & yet defying :
we are the improvised meant the moon
would bind, we lean in, slackened jaws
our lewd disguise, the ambuscade
primed to terrify vast vistas . . .

    vast vistas riddles decree

    vast vistas density deigns

I don't know this & I don't know that
but I know I'm not in Lucasville tonight
& I ain't influenced by the Ohio River
& I ain't influenced by the Scioto River
not by the Maumee nor the Muskingum of late

o but I am by the Miami's, you see, & I am
by Oahu Prison & the Cuyahoga & southern
Marin, Green Lake, the Berg upon the bluff,
the Half Note and the Vanguard, by roadhouse
jams on Austin Highway near Alamo Heights,
by every wrist-stroked torque & sighting
along a pool cue, I am influenced by lock
downs & strip searches & hardball on the
yard & my cells are blocked & my throat is
raw & I'm coughing & I've climbed aboard &
I'm nigh on somebody's ville o' Down goddamn
                    Town . . .

the frames are a fat lie hanging us
only if we live there but we don't
& we know that now, we know,
tongue/tympanum halo'd & inclusive

that we live where we listen & sound /
our rites are of empowerment
which empowerment occurs singly
which isolate dawning stands fueled
& turned definitively possible
by an ungoverned taxation we applaud

we love who we hear when we hear
each grabbed echo freed anew, alike
to our own speech when it speaks
back upon us, insisting on the effort
coming 'round again, each time
ungoverned but resonant, our spoken tax
played forth, unhomed, yet homing

painting by Cinci jazzman Jack Walker

obit for Jack Walker :
planted seed & invited taking Time

We are far from home but very unfortunate
word has just reached us here : The Last Boppers
bandmate, the SaSemble village jazz & poetry
stalwart, supremely humble jazzman and visual
artist Jack Walker (we shared a birthday, traveled
some together, shared many a stage and a few
radio broadcasts) passed away yesterday. Our
condolences to his wife Brenda, to those who
knew him as Dad, to his Lincoln Heights friends
and neighbors, to the cats he played with in the
basement at the Hirsch Recreation Center in
Cinci's Avondale neighborhood, to Napoleon who
he toured Europe with, and most especially to
Kenny, who wouldn't have had The Last Boppers
as his band's moniker had Jack not stepped up
with that name ! chills all over, Jack... you were
heard, you are loved.

The Last Boppers in the '90s
from top left, Ken Leslie, Ralph La Charity
from bottom left, Heru Lasana, Jack Walker

Kaldi's, Over the Rhine

RALPH LA CHARITY

. . .currently bills himself as a poet in private practice.
The cover collage on his earlier Dos Madres book,
litanies said handedly, and the cover collage on the
next of his Dos Madres imprints, *BLOOD VERTIGO*,
give the lie : those two books are the first two
volumes of a three-book project. This book in hand,
SPRUNGS und Alles, constitutes the concluding entry
of a trilogy he considers to be his defense of Open
Poetry readings.

www.ingramcontent.com/pod-product-compliance
Lightning Source LLC
Chambersburg PA
CBHW051143120626
46547CB00012B/922